RELENTLESS

A GOLD STAR
FATHER'S PURSUIT
OF TRUTH

⭐ KEEP ASKING ⭐

CHARLES STRANGE
&
STEVEN LEUSCHEL

Dedication

SGT Alexander J. Bennett

SPC Spencer Duncan

CWO Bryan J. Nichols

CWO David R. Carter

SSG Patrick D. Hamburger

TSgt John W. Brown

SSgt Andrew W. Harvell

TSgt Daniel L. Zerbe

PO1 (SEAL) Darrik C. Benson

CPO (SEAL) Brian R. Bill

PO1 (SEAL) Christopher G. Campbell

PO1 Jared W. Day

PO1 John Douangdara & Navy SEAL Dog "Bart"

CPO (SEAL) John W. Faas

CPO (SEAL) Kevin A. Houston

LCDR (SEAL) Jonas B. Kelsall

MCPO (SEAL) Louis J. Langlais

CPO (SEAL) Matthew D. Mason

CPO (SEAL) Stephen M. Mills

CPO Nicholas H. Null

PO1 (SEAL) Jesse D. Pittman

SCPO (SEAL) Thomas A. Ratzlaff

CPO (SEAL) Robert J. Reeves

CPO (SEAL) Heath M. Robinson

PO2 (SEAL) Nicholas P. Spehar

PO1 Michael J. Strange

PO1 (SEAL) Jon T. Tumilson

PO1 (SEAL) Aaron C. Vaughn

SCPO Kraig M. Vickers

PO1 (SEAL) Jason R. Workman

Prologue

I am an American Sailor of blood and bone,
And this body of mine is just on loan,
So, for my body you may weep,
As for my soul, it's the Lord's to keep,
I'm off to war to fight,
For a cause I feel is just and right,
Now if I should die by this foreign hand,
It will be before God, family, and homeland,
So let it be seen and known for all,
That I, Michael Strange, answered the call.

Contents

Preface

"Do your best to present yourself to God as one approved, a worker who has no need to be ashamed, rightly handling the word of truth."
-2 Timothy 2:15

IF YOUR SON, THE WORLD'S leading cryptologist, grabbed you firmly and said, *"you'll never believe what's happening in this country,"* and then died two months later, would you ask questions? If you found out the Taliban was preparing for a shootdown, and your son died in such an attack, would you want to know how the enemy was prepared? Would you stop asking questions when the Pentagon was unwilling to provide answers? If your fight led you to the White House, would you go?

Charles Strange, father of Petty Officer First Class Michael Strange, hasn't stopped asking questions and pushing the government for answers including in face-to-face meetings with multiple presidents of the United States. Charles' son Michael died in 2011 in the single largest loss of life during the Global War on Terror, on call sign Extortion 17.

The "call sign" refers to the name given to that Chinook helicopter—Extortion 17. The shootdown of that helicopter by the Taliban in Afghanistan was the largest loss of American life in the war: 30 Americans—17 SEALs, 5 DEVGRU (Naval Special Warfare Group), and 8

Army—along with 8 Afghans, and Bart the dog. For the Stranges and others, the investigation into who coordinated the downing of Extortion 17 is still open. They are in possession of 1364 pages of government documents from an investigation into Extortion 17 that suggest it was a setup tied to the bin Laden raid, opium coming to America, and other bad actors. Yet no official investigation has asked the most obvious questions.

Follow this true story of Charles Strange and his relentless pursuit of truth. His story surrounding the death of his son, Michael, and his son's comrades may change your perspective on the world. You may also feel the passion that lives within the *relentless* Charles Strange from Philadelphia, Pennsylvania.

Not only do the Stranges have *relentless* determination, they also have bona fide facts directly from the government that contradict the Department of Defense's version of the events that led to the downing of Extortion 17. Facts that they've presented to former President Donald Trump and that they state are currently under review with the Department of Justice.

This book is meant to be like an oral history, telling the Stranges' side of bin Laden raid and Extortion 17 from a Gold Star Father's perspective.

Throughout this book, pieces of the Stranges' story are triangulated with facts and evidence, including official government documents and eyewitness testimony, and statements from other parents. Note that other parents have similar stories and concerns, but this book's focus is on Charles' journey. The appendices are filled with additional information for those who are skeptical about this story and wish to better understand.

The primary purpose of *Relentless* is to gain reader support of a congressional hearing surrounding the events of call sign Extortion One

Seven. Parents, including Charles, should have the opportunity to testify and ask questions regarding the deaths of their sons.

The second purpose of *Relentless* is raise awareness of and funds for the Michael Strange Foundation. The foundation will "provide unconditional support and services to the families of recently fallen service members by professionals in several fields and also by those who have suffered similar losses so that the healing process can begin."

The Stranges' fight for truth and to help Gold Star Families continues by publishing this book. *Relentless* is intended to be an actual historical account of Charles' pursuit of truth, his work with the Michael Strange Foundation, and stories about Michael.

Introduction

"But the Lord is faithful, and he will strengthen you
and protect you from the evil one."
~2 Thessalonians 3:3

RELENTLESS CAPTURES THE STORY OF Charles Strange, Gold Star Father of Petty Officer First Class Michael Strange. Michael was killed in action on August 6, 2011, along with 29 other Americans in a helicopter crash of call sign Extortion 17. This was the largest single loss of life in the Global War on Terror and the largest loss of life to Special Operations and the Naval Warfare Group in the history of America.

Charles, Michael's father, says it hurts every day, like there's a knife in his heart. Charles and his family are so proud of Michael, his team, and our military. But, Charles still has questions surrounding the events of Extortion 17 because the evidence he possesses suggests that it was a preplanned setup linked to the bin Laden raid. He's been to Congress, the Pentagon, and the White House asking his questions, which are still, officially, unanswered.

Charles Strange

Charlie was born and raised in Philadelphia in a row house with tree-lined streets and plenty of kids to play football and other sports with around the neighborhood.

He is the grandson of Philadelphia police officer Robert Alexander, shown in Photo 1, and son of former Philadelphia police officer Charles Wesley Strange.

Photo 1. Robert Alexander, Charles' grandfather, Philadelphia Police Officer.

Charlie's grandfather helped people, his father helped people, and now Charlie, in so many different facets of his life, helps people—from the time he bought a halfway house, to the time, three weeks after Michael's death, he put his pain aside to walk an alcoholic on the streets through the 12 Steps and kindly guide him toward a better path, to relentlessly pursuing the truth of Michael's and his comrades' deaths on Extortion 17 for over a decade.

Charlie is a selfless man who yearns for the truth and loves his country.

12 Steps

When Michael was three years old, Charlie realized he needed to get sober, and he became actively involved with the 12 Steps for alcoholics for himself and Michael and his brother and sisters. Charlie's continuous sobriety started on October 15, 1989, a new life without drink or drug.

Charlie's issues with alcohol turned into hope for others as he has relentlessly helped other people suffering from the same or similar addictions since he became sober and continued his recovery.

As Charlie's friend Kurt said: "Without guys like you [Charlie], who took the time to make a guy like me, who felt all the discomfort, disease, and insanity of early sobriety, I truly wouldn't be here today living this life beyond my wildest dreams brother. The ripple effect of the men who came into my life when I was at my lowest point in life gave me the strength and hope, that I could possibly pass this gift on to another.

"I guess, like in the footsteps prayer, God carried me for a long time and delivered me into the arms of a group of drunks who did the rest. For that I will be eternally grateful. That is just a small helping of the way I feel about *Chalie*."

When Michael was young, Charlie bought a second house and turned it into a halfway house. Charlie was able to lead the halfway house effectively and bring others toward the same type of recovery he experienced. He's helped hundreds of people find a better life.

Not only was Charlie a role model for the halfway house, but his new lifestyle also became a positive influence on Michael. As a young boy, Michael would ride his 3-wheeler down the street saying, "Out of the way! I'm going to a meeting!" in reference to a 12 Step meeting with Charlie.

Michael had the opportunity to be around all sorts of people recently recovering from addiction and those with long-term recoveries through the 12 Steps.

Photo 2: Michael (left), Charlie (center), and Carly, Michael's sister, (right) on the day Michael was picked up for the Navy, going to Fort Dix.

Now, Charles still regularly attends 12 Step meetings and gets further motivation by helping new members of the program find the same recovery he continues to experience. People like Kurt became life-long friends with Charlie after Charlie helped them from their lowest points. Three decades later they continue to pass the gift of sobriety on to others.

Extortion 17's Impact

The events such as Operation Neptune Spear (the Osama bin

Laden raid), Extortion 17, and others are told from both Charles' point of view and the actual facts and statements surrounding Extortion 17.

The primary events are shown in Figure 1.

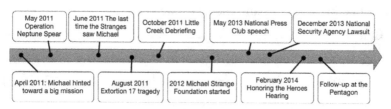

Figure 1. Extortion 17 Timeline

When Michael called Charlie in April 2011 hinting toward a big mission, Charlie never would have believed that Michael was on the team that was going to raid bin Laden's compound during Operation Neptune Spear in May 2011.

But, as the rest of the United States was celebrating bin Laden's capture and death, Michael came home in June 2011 different, seemingly tormented, following Operation Neptune Spear.

That day, June 4, 2011, he started pacing around in front of Charlie, then stopped, grabbed Charlie, and said, *"Dad, you'll never believe what's happening in this country!"* Words that scared his father and would be eventually resurface in Charlie's mind 96 days after the bin Laden raid when Michael was murdered onboard a Chinook helicopter along with 29 other Americans in August 2011.

Charlie not only had to bury his son, but he couldn't see where his son died and still doesn't know who murdered him.

In October 2011, a formal debriefing at the SEAL base in Virginia (Little Creek) left Charles and his wife, Mary, with more questions than answers. Charles has questioned everyone and everything about the events surrounding Extortion 17 including President Barack Obama, members of Congress, senators, Secretary of Defense Leon Panetta, and, later, President Donald Trump.

The paperwork the Stranges have directly from the government suggests that Extortion 17 was a preplanned setup to down SEAL Team 6. But by who, and why? The Stranges are still awaiting answers and justice in their son's and his comrades' deaths.

Out of the suffering they experience and wanting to help others through that suffering, the Stranges started the Michael Strange Foundation in 2012. The foundation's purpose is to help Gold Star Families cope with their loss, "healing the family."

Just like Charlie was able to help others through the 12 Steps, he continues to help other Gold Star Parents.

The Stranges have not backed down from asking questions about Extortion 17 and they continue to fight for truth and justice—including taking the National Security Agency to court and winning in 2013. The case went to the Supreme Court only for the laws to be changed by Congress and Obama.

In February 2014, there was a hearing called "Honoring the Heroes of Extortion 17." At that hearing, though, the most important information surrounding the mission was not permitted to be discussed. Additionally, neither Charlie nor the other parents were permitted to ask any questions or testify during the hearing, a last-minute change. As Charles seeks a real congressional hearing into Extortion 17, he also helps other families seek peace and healing.

Now, the relentless Charles Strange's mission is to help Gold Star Families because he knows the unbearable hurt that the death of a son or daughter brings to the entire family.

Read this book and you may feel the same passion for truth and justice that lives within the relentless Charles Strange. Please support a congressional hearing into Extortion One Seven and the Michael Strange Foundation.

Foreword

The Badass Michael Strange:
The Guy SEAL Team 6 Relied On

EVEN THOUGH HE FOUGHT SIDE by side with one of America's most elite and aggressive counterterrorism units, Michael Strange wasn't some Terminator-dude chiseled from Mount Rushmore who loved the smell of napalm in the morning. According to those who knew him best, he was a funny guy and, above all else, a loyal and dependable guy.

Michael Strange underwent the training, learned his skills, and deployed with SEAL Team 6 out of a simple sense of duty. Not everyone can be a cryptologist. Not everyone can be strong enough and fast enough and smart enough to go on direct action missions with a Tier 1 Unit. But Michael Strange was, and he knew it. And so, he went.

He performed his extremely complex responsibilities flawlessly on dozens of missions around the world, tracking terrorist communications in-close with the assaulters and snipers of SEAL Team 6. On August 6, 2011, Michael went on his last mission with those legendary fighters.

Around midnight, the call came in. A Ranger mission had put the enemy on the run. SEAL Team 6, along with Michael and his spy gear, were tasked with hunting them down. Michael would be needed to intercept and track the enemies' communications as they attempted to escape and coordinate a counterattack. This was real *Mission: Impossible* stuff, and it required the ability to use complex communications and encryption technology in the middle of intense firefights and other high-risk combat operations.

Tragically, as they flew through the night to support the Rangers, an enemy rocket shot down their chopper, and Michael and 29 other U.S. servicemen made the ultimate sacrifice. No one is saying Michael Strange was a Saint, but he is surely by St. Michael's side now.

For his incredibly valuable contribution to our nation's defense, Cryptologic Technician (Collection) First Class Michael Strange was awarded the Bronze Star Medal with Valor, Purple Heart Medal, Defense Meritorious Service Medal, Joint Service Commendation Medal with Valor, Joint Service Achievement Medal, Combat Action Ribbon, Presidential Unit Citation, and other campaign and unit decorations.

-Unknown

CHAPTER 1:
OPERATION NEPTUNE SPEAR

"Those who are victorious will inherit all this, and I will be their God and they will be my Children."
~Revelation 21:7

APRIL 12, 2011, TWO WEEKS before the bin Laden raid, Petty Officer First Class Michael J. Strange, a world-leading cryptologist[1] on Sea Air and Land (SEAL) Team 6 called his father, Charles Strange:

"Dad, everything's getting shut off, I'll be out of touch for a couple weeks."

"What do you mean?" Charlie asked.

"Where are you going, what are you doing?" Charlie continued prying for more information like always.

"Did the Phillies win, Dad?" asked Michael.

Before the Mission

Michael Strange—the cryptologist and son—was speaking in code to his father, "Did the Phillies win?" A code they came up with at

---

1   A cryptologist is responsible for interpreting and analyzing information and is trained in both linguistics and mathematics to both decipher and encode messages. Michael's specialty was collections.

Michael's favorite restaurant, P.F. Chang's, in Virginia Beach. While in the middle of the restaurant Charlie was trying to get information out of Michael.

Michael interrupted him and whispered, "Dad, you know who's sitting next to us?"

Charlie quickly replied, "A husband and wife, why?"

"That's what you think, Dad." And Michael changed the conversation.

When they got outside of the restaurant Michael said to Charlie, "Dad, they give me a lie detector test, like every two or three months. And the first question they ask me is when was the last time you lied?"

Charlie recognized that this, especially under a lie detector test, was a loaded question. He then understood the predicament he put Michael in as he fished for information, and what both the answers and their implications might be.

So, they came up with a code, whether it was baseball season or not. When Michael would ask, "Did the Phillies win?" it basically meant: *We need to end this conversation, start another one, and please don't ask me anymore questions about it, because I'm not permitted to discuss it.*

Michael, as a top cryptologist on SEAL Team 6, had a high-level security clearance and access to information that very few in the world did. Following the rules of secrecy was essential to keeping both the military and U.S. citizens safe.

The motto for cryptos was "Served in Silence," and that's exactly what Michael did. Many didn't even know he was on SEAL Team 6 until after his death.

Charles was always eager to learn more about Michael's new life with the SEALs but understood the need for secrecy, and now, after hearing their code phrase, he knew Michael was about to enter an extreme mission.

Photo 3: Michael at graduation with sisters Carly and Katelyn (left)
Charles (center) and his brother Chaz (right).

Michael Strange

Michael Strange was a bright yet funny kid from Philadelphia—the city of neighborhoods and brotherly love. He attended St. Bartholomew Catholic School throughout his childhood. Growing up, he liked to hang out with his friends, go to the beach with his family, and play around the neighborhood with other friends, whom he stayed close to throughout his life.

He had a way to make people laugh, whether it was imitating a comedy skit from a movie, agreeing to an outrageous dare, or joking in all kinds of situations. Michael had a knack for humor—always brightening up a group with laughter. Photos 4, 5, and 6 show Michael as a young child having fun and being silly.

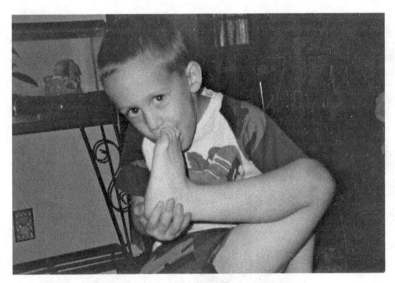

Photo 4. Michael goofing off as a young child.

Photo 5. Michael with his brother Chaz.

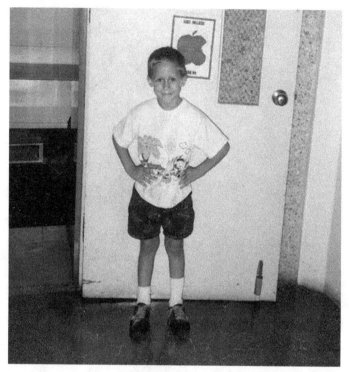

Photo 6. Michael at Lawton Elementary School, which he attended for a few years.

During his teenage years, Michael attended North Catholic High School in Philadelphia.[2] He was incredibly smart and enjoyed learning but didn't care much for school itself. He liked to work, work out at the gym, and hang out with his friends. His junior year, never having played rugby before, he decided he would learn how to play and tried out for the team, eventually becoming a star player.

As one friend, Dan Clayton, stated, "When Mike puts his mind to something, he's going to do it. Doesn't matter if he's never done it before, he's going to do it and he's going to be good at it, especially if people told him he couldn't do it."

---

2   North Catholic was the largest all-boys Catholic high school in the United States at one time. The North Catholic reunion in North Jersey has alumni fly in from all over the world.

Photo 7. Michael summiting a mountain.

He worked in the kitchen at Byrne's Tavern and in construction with his dad. Michael was an all-around great and thoughtful kid and man, always thinking of others, executing on that love, demonstrating kindness and caring, and always trying to make others laugh. Michael, seen in his North Catholic uniform next to Charlie, is shown in in Photo 8.

Photo 8. Michael (left) and Charlie (right).

Michael and his brother Chaz would help Charlie pour concrete and work construction jobs, once even taking steel from Schmidt Brewing Company and recycling it. Charlie was able to teach Michael the hard way of making money and encouraged him to go a different route in life after graduating from North Catholic High School.

Joining the Military

His senior year of high school, Michael decided to join the military, specifically the Navy, following in his Uncle Tom's footsteps. Uncle Tom and Aunt Eileen Mahoney were very close to Michael, occasionally hosting him in New England for ski trips and vacations at their house near Boston, as seen in Photos 9 and 10.

Photo 9. Michael and family touring the USS Constitution.

Photo 10. Michael and his brother Chaz snowboarding in New England.

Michael took the first steps within the military and, in 2004, graduated from basic training in Chicago.

His next step was Pensacola, Florida, to the Naval Technical Training Center and Center for Information Dominance, where he eventually took the Armed Services Vocational Aptitude Battery test or ASVAB. The Navy told everyone if they scored first place on the test, they could go anywhere they wanted. After he got the results, he called Charlie:

"Dad, they lied to me!"

Charlie remembered the time Michael went out with friends the night before his SATs and fell asleep during the actual test. But he also remembers how special Michael was, how gifted he was at a young age. "What do you mean they lied to you?"

"They told me if I got first place on the test, I could go anywhere I wanted. They lied to me, I'm not going to Virginia, I'm going to Hawaii!" said Michael in disappointment.

Michael was very close to all his family, his extended family, and the friends he grew up in Philadelphia; so, he wanted to be close to home.

"Michael, it's beautiful in Hawaii, you're going to love it!" Charlie encouraged him, while at the same time trying to hide his disappointment as well.

Michael's favorite place growing up was Rehoboth Beach, Delaware, a vacation spot for his family and the home of his grandmother. So, being on an island wasn't going to be a problem for Michael given his love for the beach.

The next time Michael called home, he described how much he loved Hawaii: "you wake up in the morning and God says, 'here's paradise.'" And Charlie had a chance to visit Michael in Hawaii, as seen in Photo 11.

Photo 11. Charlie and Michael in Hawaii.

Joining the SEALs

In that paradise, God was also calling Michael to go to DEVGRU (SEAL Team 6), the most elite SEAL Team in the world. In mid-2007, Michael was still based in Hawaii and going on missions in Iraq and Afghanistan with the Navy. The Navy SEALs approached him and wanted him to join DEVGRU (The Naval Special Warfare Development Group), so he called home to ask Charlie his opinion:

"Dad they come pick me up every day to work out with them; they want me to join the SEAL Team.[3] You know I'm not looking for a 30-year career, but I could entertain 12 years. What do you think?"

Charlie said to his son, "Well, Mikey, you know, this is your third year, going on four years. I thought you were going to do four and get out, Mikey?"

---

3   As the Global War on Terror was ramping up, more and more cryptologists were joining the SEALs to fight and be an additional asset, per an anonymous SEAL.

But Michael decided to join the SEALs. Per Charlie, many try to make it to SEAL Team 6, but less than 1% do. Michael joined SEALs, first SEAL Team 2, then SEAL Team 6 in less than four years, which is very unusual and special.

With a signing bonus in hand, Michael bought his first house in Virginia Beach near the SEAL Team 6 base, just a few short hours from his family, at 21 years old. Dual aspirations of being close to friends and family and being the best he could be were coming true.

Photo 12. Charlie and Michael in his Navy uniform.

"In May of 2009 he joined an East Coast–based SEAL team in a support role. Navy SEAL teams are known for achieving the impossible by using a unique combination of courage, competency and physical stamina to accomplish their missions. However, in addition to being competent in the combat skills needed to survive on the battlefield, these intrepid warriors also require timely critical information in order to achieve success. It was in this area that Petty Officer First Class Strange's skills and talents were applied. As a cryptologic technician, it was his job to provide and protect indispensable intelligence, intelligence that had the capacity to not only allow his team to achieve its mission, but to also save lives."[4]

Petty Officer First Class Michael Strange was a highly decorated combat veteran with numerous awards, including the Bronze Star Medal with Valor, Purple Heart Medal, Defense Meritorious Service Medal, Joint Service Commendation Medal with Valor, Joint Service Achievement Medal, Combat Action Ribbon, a Presidential Unit Citation, and other campaign and unit decorations. Michael's medals can be seen in the shadow box in Photos 13 and 14.

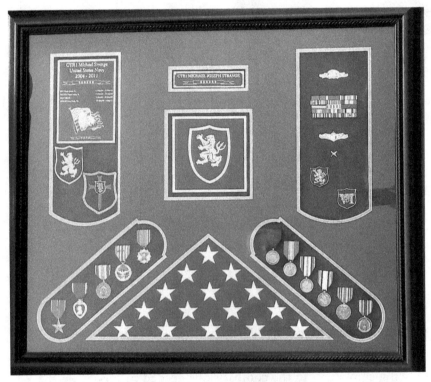

Photo 13. Michael's shadow box of awards.

Photo 14. The National Intelligence Medal for Valor. Only 17 have been given out in the history of America since World War II and the Wind Talkers.

In 2011, Michael received a Bronze Star from the President of the United States "for heroic achievement in connection with combat operations against the enemy as an Information Operations Operator for a Joint Task Force in support of Operation ENDURING FREE-DOM from June to August 2011."

"During this period, Petty Officer First Class Strange executed multiple operations and was a part of a Task Force credited with the elimination and detention of numerous enemy combatants including several high-value targets…"[5]

Photo 15: PO1 Michael Strange CTR1 on duty in Afghanistan.

On duty, Michael would go into the National Security Agency (NSA) building and two other workers would have to leave while Michael worked on the computers. The NSA workers were told "you didn't see anyone." Michael was like a kid in a candy store in the NSA building.

---

5   From the back of Michael's Bronze Star Certificate.

Above all else, though, Michael was a Strange from Philadelphia. Although he was able to travel to Africa, Bahrain, the Middle East, and other locations throughout the world, he remained dedicated and close to his family throughout his life, including during his military service. He had the same attitude at home, bringing gifts and laughter for relatives, as he did on base, selflessly helping a friend find a lost dog, and as he did in the field, attempting to save those who were mortally wounded. Michael was a funny and intelligent man, fierce warrior, and loving relative all wrapped into one.

The bin Laden Raid

So, when Michael called Charlie in April 2011, two weeks before the bin Laden raid and told him everything was getting shut off and asked about the Phillies winning almost immediately, Charlie knew Michael was about to enter deep into a mission which he could not remotely discuss.

Michael said: "Dad, if something happens, you'll hear about it."

And the raid on Osama bin Laden's compound was next, in May 2011, a mission called *Operation Neptune Spear*.

CHAPTER 2:
EXTORTION ONE SEVEN

"Fight the good fight of faith.
Take hold of the eternal life to which you were called when you made
your good confession in the presence of many witnesses."
~ 1 Timothy 6:12

WHEN MICHAEL CAME HOME IN June 2011 after the bin Laden raid, he seemed tormented. At one point at Charlie's house, he was pacing around, then he grabbed Charlie by the biceps and said *"Dad, you'll never believe what's happening in this country!"* This also alarmed Charlie, because Michael never spoke like that.

Two months later was the most devastating day in U.S. Special Operations history—Extortion 17 was shot down by the Taliban. There were 17 Navy SEALs, 5 DEVGRU members, and 8 Army men on that helicopter, call sign Extortion One Seven. All 38 men, 30 Americans and 8 Afghans, and a Navy SEAL team dog on Extortion One Seven died in the fiery crash—the largest loss of life in a single incident during the Global War on Terror.

Exposure Concerns

At the time of the bin Laden raid in May, Charlie and Mary never believed that in three short months they would be burying Michael after the largest loss of life in a single day and the largest single loss of life in the history of Naval Special Operations.[1]

Robert Gates, the secretary of defense, had reminded everyone to not release any operational details of the bin Laden raid.[2] "That commitment lasted about five hours. The initial leaks came from the White House and the CIA," according to Gates.[3]

One exposure of the SEAL team was at the Ritz-Carlton in Delaware when Vice President Joe Biden gave a speech exposing the elite team.[4] After that, Leon Panetta, director of the Central Intelligence Agency brought in Hollywood to tell the story of SEAL Team 6's bin Laden raid in the movie *Zero Dark Thirty*.

Many SEALs and their families were not happy about these leaks. "'In releasing their identity, they put a target on their backs,' said Doug Hamburger, whose son, Army Staff Sgt. Patrick Hamburger, served among the helicopter's crew."[5] Another parent thoroughly complained to their representative, who was then reported to be in Afghanistan shortly after the call. But despite the objections from families and Navy SEALs, SEAL Team 6 would be introduced to the world through Hollywood.

Hollywood

For a moment, Michael probably thought it was amusing that Leon Panetta brought in Hollywood to portray him in Operation Neptune Spear because Michael's childhood boxing coach nicknamed him *Hollywood* for his bright teeth and big smile. Michael would always ask his coach Bobby Walls—also a Philadelphia SWAT member—to spar but was told jokingly he needed to work on his defense or he would never make it to Hollywood.

Coincidently, about a few months before the bin Laden raid, SEAL Team 6 and the Philly SWAT team had an opportunity to train together. More than a decade after last seeing Coach Walls, Michael recognized him right away, nodding and smiling each time he would walk by Bobby before SEAL Team 6 and SWAT began training. Because of Michael's security clearance, he wasn't permitted to initiate conversation, so he had to wait until Bobby recognized him.

Soon thereafter:

"Holy shit! Hollywood! You're on Team 6?!" Bobby shouted to Michael.

"Well, you taught me whatever you want to be, be the best you can be. Look at you, you're a cop, you're on SWAT!"

Later, Michael joked about SEAL Team 6's upcoming training with Philly SWAT: "I know one thing, it won't be as hard as Costello's." Both Costello's—a top-tier boxing club in the nation—and Bobby had a tremendous impact on Michael becoming the best he could be— a cryptologist on SEAL Team 6.

The two were then joined at the hip for the next two weeks, working and catching up, as SEAL Team 6 and Philadelphia SWAT trained together.

So, although it may have been nice to finally tell Coach Walls that *Hollywood* made it to Hollywood—the circumstances were less than desirable.

Michael's Concerns

About a month after the bin Laden raid, in June 2011, Michael came home very different. His birthday was June 6, but he wasn't his cheerful joking self, he was very serious and seemed tormented. He was 25 years old that year.

Two days before his birthday, on June 4, 2011, Michael grabbed
Charlie by the biceps firmly and said: "***Dad, you'll never believe what's
happening in this country!***"

He then started pacing back and forth, very clearly disturbed about
something.

As the world's leading cryptologist, PO1 Michael Strange, Photo
16, knew what very few knew.

Photo 16. PO1 Michael J Strange CRT1

"Michael would often intercept a cell transmission, break the Pashtun code word of the day almost instantly and then focus in on certain ambiances: the sound of a nearby stream, a muezzin's call to *Jumu'ah* prayer, or even revving Honda motorcycles (Taliban insurgents often travel by motorcycle convoys) using some of the most sensitive headphones and listening devices in existence.

"Think of Gene Hackman's character from the classic 1974 Francis Ford Coppola thriller *The Conversation*: the taciturn surveillance and eavesdropping expert who, with his supremely trained hearing and state-of-the-art listening devices, can apply almost surreal situational awareness to recreate scenes he cannot even see.

"Using similar aptitudes, both learned and innate, Michael was able to give his brothers in SEAL Team 6 coordinates on which they could almost instantaneously vector in, proceed on foot in stealth or more explosively via Apache or Super Stallion helicopter to complete their operations." [6]

So, for someone of that caliber and security clearance to grab his father by the biceps and say *you'll never believe what's happening in this country*, when he never spoke like that, was extremely alarming and abnormal.

A Will

Looking back, Charlie remembers Michael talking about a will. And he had never talked about a will before. He told his brothers, sisters, friends, mom, and aunt that he was interested in a will, and many were alarmed that something might be happening. They never realized the details of what Michael knew and why he was so concerned about a will after the raid.

---

6   From anonymous SEAL sources

During his last time home, Michael told his Aunt Maggie that he had changed his will. He wanted a small mass, a comedian to crack jokes so no one is crying, and he wanted to be buried in Philadelphia. He also told his friend Dan how his compensation from the Navy was to be distributed, somehow hinting at his death being near. By June, Michael stated who would get what in his will.

That weekend, they had a big birthday for Michael's 25th, and the last message Charlie heard from Michael in July 2011 was "I love you Dad, I'll see you at Thanksgiving at Aunt Maggie's'" before he left again. He would never return alive.

The Shootdown

August 6, 2011, on her way to work, Mary, Charlie's wife, heard on the news that 30 Americans had died in a crash in Afghanistan. A lifelong Roman Catholic, Mary took a moment of silence and prayed for those on board who lost their lives, and their families. Little did she know she was already praying for her stepson Michael.

A few minutes later, while Mary was on I-95, Charlie's sister Maggie called her wondering where Charlie was, and asked that Mary go home, because something bad had happened to Michael. Michael was very close to Aunt Maggie, who treated him like her own. Mary, though, still didn't connect the dots between the crash in Afghanistan and something bad happening to Michael and his comrades.

She immediately went through the grass embankment, sped on I-95, blew threw a red light, and arrived back home to hear the most horrible sound she had ever heard. She didn't know what it was until she saw her son, Drew, on the ground bear-hugging Charlie. Charlie had just gotten the call about Michael's death from Charlie's daughter Katelyn.

Charlie's fresh tattoo of the American flag was bleeding from him banging it off the fence and screaming that moment he found out that Michael had perished in Afghanistan. Drew was on ground with Charlie holding him, and from the look in his eyes, Mary knew that he needed help comforting Charlie.

"He's gone! He's dead!" Charlie gave out a scream when he saw Mary.

She then realized that the news about the crash in Afghanistan had to have included Michael.

"What happened? What happened?" Mary asked as she ran to Charlie and took over Drew's position in attempting to comfort him.

"I don't know, I don't know…" Charlie could barely get the words out of his mouth as he continued to cry and scream in agony.

And that's when the questioning began. What happened to their beloved Michael and the others on board that Chinook? A question that would lead them to the Pentagon, to the White House, and on a journey to helping Gold Star Families cope with the loss of their sons and daughters.

The Stranges then drove to Michael's mother's house and met with three gentlemen—Casualty Assistance Calls Officers (CACOs). Like most CACOs, it was their first time, so despite Charlie's multiple attempts at asking them what happened, they were unable to answer because they too didn't know any details of the crash. Other military members were there, giving their account of what they were told happened.

Later, Charlie heard about the crash on the news. The news reiterated the same story along with President Obama's[7] plan to meet the families in Dover:

"President Obama paid tribute today to the 30 U.S. troops killed over the weekend in Afghanistan and he vowed to press on there and

---

7   President Obama also sent a letter and a note, found in Appendix B and C.

succeed. The Americans including 22 SEALs were killed when their helicopter was shot down in Wardak province. David Martin reports:

"Their remains will be flown tomorrow to Dover Air Force Base in Delaware...It will take two transport planes to bring all the flag draped caskets home. 30 Americans were aboard that Chinook helicopter when it went down. A crash so horrific that remains have not yet been identified. A shocking loss for the nation...

"The SEALs aboard the Chinook were assigned to back up another team which had hit a compound in the Tangi Valley west of Kabul looking for a local Afghan leader. The team got pinned down in a firefight and called for help. The Chinook with 30 Americans, eight Afghans and one dog aboard was apparently hit by a rocket propelled grenade as it came in.

"A Taliban commander told CBS News, 'The man the SEALs were looking for wasn't there. We had all our forces in position to defend our Valley' he said, 'the commander is alive and well.'

"Earlier this afternoon the aircraft carrying the Americans took off from Afghanistan for the final journey home. They will arrive at Dover Air Force Base in Delaware tomorrow morning."[8] [6]

Dover

On August 18, 2011, about two weeks after Extortion 17, President Obama met the families as their loved ones were being brought back into the United States in caskets, as shown in Photo 15.[9] It was a harrowing experience—to see so many different caskets, parents dropping to their knees and crying as they arrived.

---

8   This is not the specific news story Charlie heard that morning, but this story came on the news shortly thereafter.

9   Bill Littner, who assisted with the caskets and helps regularly with the Michael Strange Foundation, claims the official narrative was and is filled with falsehoods and bad decisions, but he doesn't know why.

When the caskets were coming in, Katelyn, Charles' daughter, saw a different flag and asked, "Dad, who's flag is that?"

"That's the Afghanistan flag."

"What are they doing here?" screamed Katelyn.

The Stranges learned later that the military didn't know who the Afghans were because the seven Afghans were switched out and the names didn't match the manifest.

Photo 17. Caskets from Extortion 17 being sent to Dover.

President Obama

President Obama was walking down the line giving condolences to all the family members. Obama made his way to Charlie and attempted to comfort Charlie. Obama, grabbing Charlie's shoulders, said, "Michael changed the way America lives." Charlie assumed Obama was talking about the bin Laden raid. He continued to talk about Michael.

Charlie then grabbed President Obama by the shoulders, shook him, and sternly said: "I don't need to know *about* my son, I need to know ***what happened*** to my son."

President Obama's head went back and immediately the Secret Service grabbed Charlie and removed President Obama from the situation.

Later, President Obama came up to Charlie again and hugged him. At that time, Charlie pushed on Obama once more saying, "Is there going to be a congressional hearing, Mr. President?"

Obama said, with his lips next to Charlie's ear, "We'll look into it, very, very, very deep." The Stranges haven't heard anything from President Obama since.

Leon Panetta

A bit later, Leon Panetta came up to Charlie, shook his hand, and he said, "Mr. Strange, I'm going to ask some of the same questions you're asking."

Charlie, in disbelief, said "I'm a blackjack dealer from Philadelphia—and you're going to ask the same questions I'm asking? Are you serious?"

According to the Stranges, many of the families felt something was wrong. Once Charlie spoke up, some of the other father's started to jump in, as Secret Service once again grabbed Charlie and removed him from Leon Panetta.

Becoming a Gold Star

No father should ever have to bury his son. But on August 6, 2011, Charles became a Gold Star[10] Father, and he had no choice but to bury his son Michael. It became extremely difficult for Charlie and his family to find peace with the unknown circumstances surrounding Michael's death and now his burial.

---

10   A Gold Star Family is defined as a family who has lost a loved one in service to our country in a time of war.

Unnecessary Cremation

In the report and on the news all over the world, an Army Ranger Sergeant talked about 38 skulls and c-spines at the crash, meaning that all bodies had been completely burned to death and were unrecognizable. Col. David Lapan and Captain Jane Campbell from the Pentagon stated this as well. The news also said the *crash was so horrific that remains have not yet been identified*. Additionally, two Navy representatives informed Michael's parents that he was burnt so badly, they believed they had no other choice but cremation. So, that's what they decided to do.

However, when Charlie requested the autopsy report in December 2011 from Dover, the photos showed that Michael was not burnt and the hair on his arms could actually be seen, therefore he could have had a traditional Catholic burial with an open casket funeral.[7] It was an error or lie that still haunts Michael's family to this day.

Michael's Funeral

Michael's service and funeral mass were at the Cathedral Basilica of Saints Peter and Paul in Center City, Philadelphia, shown in Photos 16 and 17. There were snipers on the roof, military members[11] present to honor Michael, flags at half-mast, and friends crowded into the cathedral.

It was beautiful celebration of Michael's life, which had ended far too soon. Bobby Crawford from the Warriors' Watch Riders, who brought Michael back from Dover to Philadelphia, was there along with the Patriot Guard Riders. Additionally, about 100 military members were present as well as representatives and senators. Many people

---

11 One childhood friend—a Green Beret—was dressed and ready to go to the funeral but chose to miss the funeral because no one should have sent those men on that mission. He was fearful that, seeing other military, he couldn't keep his mouth shut at the funeral.

Charlie didn't even know from the area came to pay their respects to Michael and his family.

Photo 18: Cathedral Basilica of Saints Peter and Paul in Philadelphia

Photo 19. Outside the cathedral in Center City, Philadelphia.

Philadelphia has a strong support system as the city lost many men in Vietnam. Specifically, Thomas Edison and Father Judge High Schools in Philadelphia lost the most men in the country in the Vietnam War.[8] So, the veterans and families of Philadelphia understand the pain of losing a son in war and came to support the Stranges.

Snipers were on the roof to protect the families from attacks, since the Taliban had threatened to wipe out the bloodlines of all SEAL Team 6 members. Coincidently, there was an explosion at the Fraternal Order of Police (FOP) office, where Michael's reception was to be held, a day or two before the funeral.

The funeral itself was a beautiful and honorable but very painful day. They then buried Michael in Arlington, with 17 of the 30 men.

Friends and family still go to Arlington nearly every year to celebrate Michael's life. Photos are shown in Photos 21–30.

Charlie, though, still had no closure on Michael's death because he still didn't know what happened to his son in that horrific helicopter crash known by its call sign: Extortion One Seven.

Photo 20. Extortion 17 drawn by Bill Littner
in the uniform he wore bringing Michael and others back to Dover.

Photo 21. Michael as a young boy.

Photo 22. Michael, Charlie, and Michael's prom date Santina.

Photo 23. Charlie and Michael at Michael's graduation.

Photo 24. Michael.

Photo 25. Michael.

Photo 26. Michael with his niece Juliana.

Photo 27. Katelyn, Juliana, Chaz, and Michael.

Photo 28. Michael's headstone at Arlington National Cemetery.

Photo 29. Charlie at Arlington with Michael.

Photo 30. Michael's mural, donated by Zack Byrd, in Port Richmond on the side of Celtic Shirts at Belgrade and Clearfield streets in Philadelphia, just a few minutes from the Rocky steps at the Philadelphia Art Museum.

CHAPTER 3:
LITTLE CREEK DEBRIEFING

"A time to love and a time to hate, a time for war and a time for peace."
~Ecclesiastes 3:8

ON OCTOBER 12, 2011, AT 5 a.m., Charlie and Mary packed up the car and traveled down I-95 toward Virginia Beach, Virginia. They were both anxious and eager about how the next two days would unfold and the truth they may find during the debriefing.

Brigadier General Jeffrey Colt had investigated the events of Extortion 17 for a month, including two weeks with boots on the ground in Afghanistan, a country about the size of Texas. The debriefing in Little Creek near Virginia Beach was to inform the families of his findings. Charles and Mary hoped for closure, but, after these two days and the information provided, they left with only more questions about what really happened.

Journey to Little Creek

Little Creek was established during World War II, a combination of four bases: Camp Bradford, Camp Shelton, U.S. Naval Frontier

Base, and Amphibious Training Base. In 2009, the Joint Expeditionary Base Little Creek-Fort Story was established.

Each of the families of the victims of Extortion 17 received a letter inviting them to Virginia for Colt's debrief. Brigadier General Jeffrey Colt was the Commander, Joint Unmanned Aircraft Systems Center of Excellence for the U.S. Army Joint Forces Command at Creech Air Force Base and the Deputy Commanding General for the 101st Airborne Division (Air Assault) from February 2011 to June 2012.

Note: Air Force Captain Joni Marquez was the fire control officer aboard the AC-130 gunship that Army Rangers called for support. Captain Marquez claims the Pentagon hid the truth and lied about the circumstances that led to Extortion 17. Captain Marquez was denied authorization to fire 6 times, when Michael was alive for 10–20 minutes. She gave Charlie handwritten notes on Colt's summary report that contradicted the General's account. One of those notes is shown in Appendix D.

Meeting of the Families

Military friends, high-ranking government workers, and others were already questioning the narrative that Charlie and Mary were told. They suggested that the couple talk to other parents to triangulate the story and get more facts and information surrounding Extortion 17.

So, after checking into the one of two hotels where parents of Extortion 17 were, they became increasingly eager to speak to other parents. Mary wrote a letter and left it at the front desk for other parents to see. It read:

Any families from Extortion 17 that would like to meet the Strange family, meet in the lobby at 7 p.m.

After reading the note and speaking to Charles, the hotel was gracious enough to offer a conference room for the families of Extortion 17 to meet.

At about 6:15 p.m., Charles and Mary went to the lobby and began meeting and greeting other parents and those who came in for Colt's investigation debriefing. About 18 other parents joined them in the conference room and they began to speak.

Each set of parents introduced themselves and talked about their sons and how they heard the news of Extortion 17. With only two months after their sons were buried, the parents were still suffering and grieving, but they remembered what they were told about their son's death.

Some were told the helicopter crashed into the side of a mountain, others were told the Chinook had a mechanical failure. To the Stranges, it seemed that each family in the room had been told a different story about what happened that day.

By this time, however, everyone had come with the understanding that the Chinook was shot down by the Taliban, but they did not know the facts surrounding the shootdown.

After the informal get together, the parents went back to their rooms, preparing for the events of the next day and hoping Brigadier General Jeffrey Colt's findings would bring closure.

Colt's Findings

The next morning, a coach bus came to both hotels to pick up the parents and drive them to Little Creek. After about a 20-minute ride, the bus parked, and the parents were instructed to walk toward what was a movie theater–like area.

Before entering, Charles and Mary were greeted by someone in the military who said: "That was very nice last night, getting all the parents together."

"Thank you, yes it was just to get everyone together to see how everyone's doing…," Charles reluctantly responded.

But Charles and Mary looked at each other, and both immediately thought, "how did they even know?"

From then on, the Stranges were separated from the other families and escorted via a large blacked-out sport utility vehicle. They would have two dedicated government officials tailing them for the rest of the debriefing and for all future memorial services. The Stranges believe that these government officials wanted to know what the Stranges knew and kept them purposefully separated from the other families. To this day, the Navy SEAL Foundation does not invite the Stranges to events.

Theater

As they entered the theater, each group of parents selected a seat and turned their attention to the military members present: Admiral Harwood, Brigadier General Colt, a few Navy JAGs, and other young men in Navy.

The first portion of this time in the theater started off with the pilots—how and why they were qualified to fly the Chinook into the Tangi Valley of Afghanistan. The main pilot, Chief Warrant Officer David Carter, had extensive hours in Iraq, which Colt used to explain Carter's flight of the Chinook in Afghanistan.

After taking approximately 40 minutes explaining the flight and the terrain, the lights began to dim in preparation for the short video. Darkness filled the theater. Silence. Then parents began to hear radio chatter…then…firepower. The Stranges remember this being an emotionally tormenting experience for many—reliving the death of their sons.

"We have a fallen angel! Fallen angel!" referring to the Chinook being shot down.

Emotion struck the room. Parents were in tears, others groaning, some running out of the room in despair. It was a devastating experience. The Stranges believed it was pure cruelty to put the families through the death of their loved ones again, especially in that fashion. The Stranges also believe this was purposeful to cause psychological damage so the families wouldn't ask any substantiative questions. Many parents couldn't even go back in, they were so devastated.

Lucky Shot

Colt then stated that the 100-yard shot in the dark was a "lucky shot," as the video ended.

Charlie stood up abruptly and yelled, "What did he say?! Did you say lucky fuckin' shot?!"

Charlie continued yelling: "All our sons are dead! Lucky shot!? Are you kidding me? Lucky would have been if they missed!"

Brigadier General Colt put his head down in silence.

"What is this? Are we playing a basketball or hockey game? A lucky shot? Give me a break!"

Charlie paused as he saw the JAGs walk toward him.

Black Box

"What happened to the black box!?" Charlie shouted another question.

General Colt raised his hands in the air, "a flash flood came and washed it away," he said as he motioned his hands like a raging river washing away the black box. He explained that the nearby dam broke and washed the orange box away from the crash scene, unable to be found.

He then stated they looked for the black box and could hear the beacon, but they never found it.[12]

---

12 A month later, Charlie learned from someone at command that the Chinook had no black box. And later, they learned that there must be a recording device by law. There is still confusion around the existence of a black box on Extortion 17.

Then one of the Navy members grabbed the back of Charlie's shoulders to escort him out of the room to calm down. As they were walking out, Charlie continued:

"Something's wrong here! This is bullshit! Who's really in charge?!" Charlie shouted, questioning the narrative.

Why a Chinook

"Why were they in a Chinook and not a Blackhawk?" one of the parents shouted, referencing the differences in agility and purpose of Chinooks versus Blackhawks, as shown in Figures 2 and 3.

Figure 2: A Chinook helicopter.

Figure 3: A Blackhawk helicopter.

"You put our sons in a school bus! They were a sitting target!" Charlie shouted.

The Naval officers attempting to calm him down said: "It doesn't matter what helicopter they were in, it would have fallen regardless the way it was hit. The RPG hit the propeller and the g-force killed them all."

Charlie, even more emotional, told the JAG to "I'm going to knock your teeth down your throat," now attributing the lies to the JAG himself. *The Stranges later learned from a military family member that the probability of enough momentum building up in a Chinook 100 feet off the ground to create enough g-forces to kill men was virtually impossible.*

"You mean to tell me that a Chinook is the same as a Blackhawk? Who's running this war? You guys look like you've never even been in a slap fight!"

Visibly and verbally extremely upset, Charlie was then finally escorted outside.

After a bottle of water and calming down outside, Charlie went back into the theater. He and others asked if they could watch the video again, and their questions became more articulate.

After watching the mostly black video of some bullets flying and eventually a ball of fire simulating the Chinook shoot down, Charlie knew enough about RPGs to know the chances of shooting down a Chinook from 100 yards away, in the pitch dark, were extremely low. Thus, the chances of this story being truth were also extremely low.

"Ya know," Charlie started, "an RPG hitting the Chinook's propellers at that distance is like dropping a quarter from the top of the Empire State Building and landing it in a coffee cup." The 1364 pages mention MANPADs (Man Portable Defense System) several times, so Charlie believes the Chinook may have been shot down by a more accurate and targeted MANPAD. And he believes the seven Afghans on board may have had something to do with the downing of Extortion 17. The attack on Benghazi, which happened 13 months after Extortion 17, involved MANPADS.

Rules of Engagement

Another father asked a question, "Why was there no return fire on the enemy once the RPGs had been launched?"[9]

"To win the hearts and minds. There could have been civilians there," stated Admiral Harwood said referencing the rules of engagement.[13]

Charlie, frustrated, now believed that this debrief event wasn't meant to disclose the truth; it seemed more like a psychological operation, or psyops. They learned later from Gary Reid at the Pentagon that the audio was fabricated for effect in telling the story.

At that point, the questioning was over, and it was time to leave the theater and go to SEAL Team 6's base, where no civilian had ever been.

---

13   *Rules of Engagement* are military directives describing the circumstances that military can enter and continue combat with opposing forces.

SEAL Team 6 Base

The team room for the SEALs was about ¾ of a football field, with a big bar against the wall. Knives, guns, and hatchets laced the walls. The chandeliers were made out of machine guns— an exciting sight for even non-gun enthusiasts. Charlie looked down on the table to see awards, write-ups, and medals—a section for each person killed in Extortion 17.

One of the awards was The Defense Meritorious Service Medal. The certificate read:

"Petty Officer First Class Michael J. Strange, United States Navy, distinguished himself by exceptionally meritorious service as an Information Operations Detachment Leading Petty Officer and Squadron Direct Support Enabler from 28 May 2009 to 6 August 2011.

"During this period, Petty Officer Strange's aggressive leadership, extraordinary professionalism, unmatched technical skill, and sustained superior performance had direct positive impact on National-level strategic exercises and contributed to his command's overall mission success. A seasoned cryptologist and enabler, he was instrumental in the development and fielding of cutting-edge ground and maritime signals intelligence tactics, techniques, and procedures, directly contributing to the commander's ability to conduct operations and revitalized afloat cryptology in the special operations force environment.

"Petty Officer First Class Strange's unwavering dedication and effectiveness was unmatched. In the dedication of his service to his country and through his distinctive accomplishments, Petty Officer First Class Strange reflected great credit upon himself, the Joint Special Operations command, the United States Navy, and the Department of Defense."

Charlie, wiping the tears from his eyes, looked up and saw that

Admiral Shaffer was at the bar in the team room with a young man who looked like a 3-star admiral and another young man.

"Michael Strange's dad, it's nice to meet you! Michael was great. I'm so sorry about his death. We dropped bombs, we got them..." he emotionally stated.

But the metaphorical bombs had already been dropped on Michael's circle. Michael was like a nucleus of his closest friends and family—the glue that kept his friends together. Whether it be around special events like the prom or one of Michael's rugby games, or just his shenanigans at parties and get-togethers, Michael had a special way of keeping his friends and family more connected than they would ever be without him.

General Colt then grabbed Admiral Shaffer, turned him around, and walked him away from Charlie. It seemed Shaffer was drinking, knew the guys including Michael, and was emotionally hurt by the deaths of Extortion 17. Charlie was led the other way as General Colt stated, "come with us." The Stranges went back to the bus and eventually back to Philadelphia.

Before departing, though, they were handed a folder with 25 pages and a compact disc (CD). Some of the parents stated the plan was they were going to ask for the CD back.

That day, Charlie and Mary drove back to Philadelphia wondering what had just happened. They expected to get more answers but became more emotionally upset and had more questions. Questions like why were they in a Chinook? How does g-force kill everyone so near the ground? How can an RPG travel a hundred yards and hit the Chinook in the perfect spot to cause mass destruction?

Things weren't adding up for the Stranges.

Once discovered, the contents of that CD would lead Charles and Mary down another pathway toward the truth, giving them ammunition to ask much more very specific questions.

CHAPTER 4:
1364 PAGES

"Put on the full armor of God,
so that you can take your stand against the devil's schemes."
~ Ephesians 6:11

BLANK PAGES. THAT'S WHAT CHARLIE found when he opened up the folder from Little Creek. Blank pages! Technically, the first two pages did have some ink, but the rest were completely blank. And placed next to the blank pages in that folder the Stranges received was a CD that was barely accessible—it was completely encrypted.

But Mary figured out how to access the disc and retrieve the files, which would give the couple far more ammunition to ask questions than any of the previous revelations combined. It would also cause the couple to have a target on their backs from various government agencies—presumably for trying to expose the truth.

Accessing the Pages

When Charlie saw the pages were blank, he called Vice Admiral Sean Pybus, Commander and Chief of Central Command.[14]

---

14   Charlie believes this goes above Central Command to bad actors in the U.S. government.

"Admiral Pybus, hi, its Charles Strange."

"Hi, Mr. Strange, how can I help you?"

"Well, I got a bad copy, and I can't read it… seems as though only the first two pages had print on it and the rest are blank," Charlie questioned.

"Well, Mr. Strange, we received a lot of complaints about that…"

"Well, can you send me another one?" Asked Charlie.

"No, sorry, we can't…"

"Why not?" Charlie was starting to get angry.

"…We burned it…" Pybus answered.

The conversation quickly ended with Vice Admiral Pybus.

Confused, yet eager, Charlie turned to the disc and popped it into a computer. He tried to find files, but he couldn't figure it out, only seeing blocks, and when he clicked on the blocks nothing happened. So, Mary took over.

Mary, with an energy drink in hand and obsessive-compulsive disorder kicking into full effect, began clicking, holding, and trying to decipher the disc. She wasn't planning on stopping until she was able to access whatever information may exist on the disc regarding Extortion 17 and Michael's and his comrades' deaths.

What Mary saw were all types of little blocks, and when she clicked on the blocks they turned into a bubble. After a few hours, Mary realized less blocks were coming up. She concluded there was some type of pattern, a code she needed to decrypt. Michael probably could have cracked the encryption in seconds, so Mary used his inspiration to continue onward.

After eight hours, she could finally see words and sentences. She started to read and realized it was the first page of Colt's investigative findings. The couple then had the same excitement that PO1 Michael Strange experienced as a cryptologist on SEAL Team 6.

Charlie was told from other SEALs that Michael would focus and concentrate when determining a location of a terrorist, and other SEALs would stand around him, forming a perimeter. When Michael finally located the target, he would jump up and shout, "Let's go! Let's go get those fuckin' squirters!!" in excitement with his Philly attitude.

Now, Charlie and Mary felt that same exact excitement from cracking the encrypted disc.

The couple began to quickly read the pages on the computer. They soon realized the amount of information was far beyond what they were led to believe during Colt's debriefing. The disc contained raw data from Colt's investigation that painted a very different picture of the events surrounding Extortion 17.

They printed out a hard copy on paper in case they lost the electronic file or it became corrupted.

The printer kept printing and printing. There were so many pages the couple had to go get more paper and more ink to continue printing the stacks of pages—1364 pages in all.

Once they started reading the pages beyond the summary report, emotion struck the Stranges' house. The couple was angry, crying, and angry again. To the Stranges, General Colt's summary report was not an accurate summary of the 1364 pages.

The pages contained data and evidence collected by Brigadier General Colt, including interviews and statements from those involved in the operation. Even just briefly looking through all the pages, they realized the detailed information was left out of General Colt's summary report. When pieced together into an actual investigation, the information made it clear to them that *Extortion 17 was a setup*.

Charlie turned around and looked at Mary and said: "This is all by design. It was a complete setup."

Mary agreed.

The couple were frustrated, crying, and extremely emotional realizing that Michael may have put trust into the people who were responsible for his death. Charles and Mary are shown in Photo 31 with some the 1364 pages.

Photo 31. Charles and Mary with the 1364 pages.
Photo from the Philadelphia Inquirer.

Protecting the Information

Picking each other up from the emotional nightmare they found in these pages, the Stranges realized the information they had was precious. So, they printed more copies and stored those in various locations with notes stating they are of sound mind and body and have no interest in killing themselves.

The couple wrote a letter to Billy and Karen Vaughn with instructions on how to decrypt the disc and download the report. They were sure to do this by mail, as they were afraid to discuss it via email or phone. Then, they told another family how to do it.

Through the 1364 pages, they came to the realization that the shootdown of Extortion 17, and the entire mission, was all by design. It was a setup linked to bin Laden (as stated in the documents). But by who and why?

Evidence of a Setup

Charlie and Mary learned many details, like there were six improvised explosive devices at the landing site and on the way there. Charlie believes that this was so no one could come right in to help if anyone was alive. There were no lights, no fire pits[15] that lit up the village, leading Charlie to believe that the village knew. So many coincidences.

They also learned that on May 11, 2011—9 days after the bin Laden raid—100 Taliban were coming to the Tangi valley to shoot down the coalition aircraft. There are so many points indicating that Extortion 17 was a setup, including the Taliban on the roof with RPG's and under trees with night vision goggles, motorcycles, and machine guns, just waiting for SEAL Team 6.

This evidence suggests that the Taliban not only knew the SEALs were coming, but they were prepared to take down the Chinook in multiple scenarios. Even scarier, the Stranges learned that decisions were rushed and "hands were tied from above."

100 Taliban Traveled to the Tangi Valley

One person interviewed in the 1364 pages stated that there was a brief report from May 11, 2011 (less than 10 days after the bin Laden raid) that "over 100 Taliban traveled from the [redacted] Province to the Tangi Valley to shoot down the coalition force aircraft."[16] It also

---

15   Charlie knows that everyone in that area of the Tangi Valley had to know what was going to happen for them not to have their fire pits in front of their houses that night.

16   This section of the 1364 pages can be found in Appendix E.

says in the 1364 pages that the Taliban was hoping the coalition would send in more troops—that's how prepared they were for the shoot-down.

Additionally, less than 30 minutes after the shootdown, the Taliban were bragging on the internet that they just killed SEAL Team 6. And by no coincidence, Hamid Karzai, the president of Afghanistan, was the first person to mention it on national television. How did they know who was on the Chinook? Another coincidence.

These two pieces of evidence imply that the Taliban may have known about Extortion One Seven almost immediately following the bin Laden raid and knew they were targeting SEAL Team 6. This suggests that there may have been insider involvement and the shootdown may have been linked to the bin Laden raid.

No Afghans Interviewed

Throughout the entire 1364 pages, one thing seemed to be missing: interviews from Afghans. Despite being in Afghanistan for two weeks, Jeffrey Colt seems to have not interviewed one Afghan about what happened that night. This seems unusually odd given the evidence suggesting the Afghans were prepared and that the entire valley knew something was happening, based on the lack of fires that night.

One person interviewed stated that "Insurgents may have been receiving information about coalition forces' movement from at least one local resident."[17] But yet again, no Afghans were interviewed and asked about that local resident.

Rangers out of Danger

The original story of Extortion 17's mission was that a team of Army Rangers were in danger and pinned down in a firefight. How-

---

17   This full statement can be found in Appendix F.

ever, the aircraft commander, whose interview was published in the 1364 pages, stated, "from our perspective, the ground team was not in any danger."[18]

The Rangers being out of danger means that Extortion 17 should have never been sent in the first place. The original story was that the Rangers were in danger, but it then changed to the SEALs being after a high-value target, Qari Tahir.

Rushed Decisions

One series of interviews stated that "it just appeared to us the whole plan for getting into this area was rushed... for three hours we had been burning holes in the sky. You've got AWT [Army Warrior Tasks] flying around, so there's a lot of noise going on and basically, the entire valley knows there's something happening in the area . . . by the time we've been there for three hours, and the party's up, bringing in another air-craft like that [a Chinook] you know, may not be the most tactically sound decision."[19]

This statement implies that it was not a tactically sound decision to send a Chinook into an area like an active battle zone. Why not split them up and put them in more maneuverable Black Hawk helicopters?

No Eyes on Extortion 17

Charlie learned that there were three eyes in the sky, or cameras available, to watch Extortion 17. However, all three had glitches and went down the exact moment Extortion 17 was shot down. Additionally, command didn't know for ten minutes that Extortion 17 had gone down.[20]

---

18 The full statement can be read in Appendix G.
19 This full set of interviews can be found in Appendix I.
20 These statements can be read in Appendix J.

The most elite team in the world—SEAL Team 6—who all eyes were on months earlier during the bin Laden raid are now dead? And all the available cameras had glitches simultaneously? And Central Command didn't know Extortion 17 was hit and downed for ten minutes? What was happening during those ten minutes? There are too many coincidences.

The report didn't answer those questions.

The Stranges formulated questions that presumably should have been asked by General Colt in his investigation but weren't. Many of the questions point toward insider involvement and Extortion 17 being set up. Now, conflicting information direct from the government raises the questions, *"What really happened? And, why?"*

Questions from the 1364 Pages

From the 1364 pages and surrounding information, Charles and Mary formulated several questions. What follows are the actual questions they developed.

- The Tangi Valley is known to be the Taliban stronghold; why land them in a landing zone that had never been used before, only observed through satellites?

- The seven Afghan commandos who were originally on Extortion 17 either got off and refused to get back on the chopper OR were switched out and seven new Afghans got on board. Who made this decision? Why? Why did General Colt not ask this question?

- Why were the original seven Afghans never questioned?

- The night vision goggles (NVG) weren't working for our troops, but they worked for the Taliban. Why?

- Upon landing, the pilot gives a 3-minute call and a 1-minute call, except the time frame during which these calls were made gives a lapse of 13 minutes. What was going on during that time?

- We were told the black boxes washed away in a flash flood. These boxes [or recording devices] are almost indestructible, and they are built with a beacon that can be found 14 miles into the ocean. What's on that box that the military and/or the government does not want us to hear?

- There were three eyes in the sky but not one on Extortion 17. Why? General Colt asks about them and is told "We NEVER did a mission like this sir [referring to General Colt], it made us feel very vulnerable. Our hands were tied from up above." How far is up above? Who gave this command?

- We were told on October 12, 2011, by General Colt that a Taliban "low-level fighter" shoots a rocket propelled grenade (RPG) [was it a MANPAD?] from approximately 100 yards in pitch black and got a lucky shot because it hit the aft blade, the rear blade, which then caused Extortion 17 to go into a horrible, violent spin. Then, it exploded in air, exploded when it went nose down then exploded again due to all the ammo on board, since it was SEAL Team 6. The chopper was so hot (from the live ammo) it couldn't be approached for 24 hours. Well, there are conflicting reports as to how long before it could be approached to identify all on board. Why were there conflicting reports? Which is true?

- October 12, 2011, General Colt states that all 38 men were killed from g-forces. How much g-force can you get at 100–150 feet above ground?

- Navy Captain Jane Campbell and Marine Colonel David Lapan, both are spokespersons for the Pentagon, gave reports that "no identifiable remains" and "38 c-spines and skulls are all that remain" at the site of the crash. Why?

- We requested Michael's autopsy report and inside was also a disc which contained the pictures of Michael. My son was completely intact except for his right ankle, which was badly damaged. But they said he was "burnt beyond recognition." They cremated Michael when he did not need to be. Michael still had hair on his arms. How hot was this chopper?

- In the papers, it says the Rangers were in no danger; America was told it was a rescue mission to save the Rangers. Why?

CHAPTER 5:
BATTLING THE NSA

"You are my war club, my weapon for battle—with you I shatter nations, with you I destroy kingdoms."
-Jeremiah 51:20

ONCE THEY HAD THE PAGES, all 1364 of them, and understood enough of the contents, things started to get more serious in their battle for truth. After unwanted phone calls, text messages, and photographs, the Stranges had enough and took their issues up with the court.

The next battle ended with the Stranges beating the National Security Agency and the Obama administration in one of the highest courts in the United States. But even that did not cause enough attention to get answers as to why Michael was killed.

Text Messages

Charlie started receiving text messages from 001 and 000 and Mary was getting them from 73256. They tried responding several times with no avail. Some messages he received were simply the numbers 73256. After a few of them from the same two numbers, Charlie called Verizon and told them the story.

"Do you know who's texting me?" Charlie asked.

"Yeah…" said the Verizon operator.

"No who is it?" Charlie asked again.

"Yeah…" The operator said once again, reluctantly.

"Sir, do you know who that is?" Charlie asked again.

"Yeah…Big brother is watching you…" The Verizon operator then hung up quickly thereafter.

Charlie wasn't happy, but he wasn't surprised.

Later, one of Michael's friends pointed out that the message 73256 can be translated to SEAL6 using the letters on a phone's keypad. So, was it the government harassing Charlie, or was it the SEALs somehow letting Charlie and Mary know they support him?

There was no doubt that Michael took his same personality over to the SEALs, a personality of both humor and sincere caring, for which many people who met him instantly loved him. So, for Charlie to feel the same support from others that knew Michael is not out of the question.

Michael had a way of making many friends, but he kept his closest friends even closer. At Michael's funeral there must have been 50 people that came up to Charlie and said Michael was their best friend. Michael was somehow able to influence nearly everyone he came in contact with—whether it be through laughter or drive to succeed or courage.

SEAL Support

Charlie and Mary had the opportunity to meet with two of the original SEAL Team members at a dinner in Virginia for Honor and Remember Flag. They looked like offensive linemen, and they were the nicest, funniest guys. Their wives were with them, and the couples had a great night joking and conversing.

Later at that dinner, an admiral interrupted the conversation: "Mr. Strange, there's two men from SEAL Team 6 that would like you meet you outside." So, Charlie followed him out of the dining room to a hallway where he was introduced to the SEALs.

"What an honor to meet you, Mr. Strange. We served with Michael."

"Thank you, it's nice to meet you both."

They then proceeded to talk about Michael, reminiscing with Charlie. One story was about Michael's Trump shower shoes. Apparently, Michael would always shower in his Trump flip-flops, as he was a fan of the businessman at that time prior to 2011. Charlie remembers him and Michael getting the sandals in Trump Plaza at Atlantic City, near their home in Philadelphia. They all laughed, and Charlie cried about those few minutes they were able to remember and talk about Michael together.

At the end of the conversation, they shook Charlie's hand again firmly and one said, *"never stop asking questions, Mr. Strange, never stop asking questions."* The request still motivates him today as he battles for truth.

A Virus and Photograph

But not everyone supported Charlie and Mary's quest for truth. A few days after Mary discovered the 1364 pages, she was relaxing—playing games on the computer and reading some articles when a photo popped up on her screen. Her computer froze with the photo, seen in Photo 32, unable to be closed. She looked at the photo more closely and realized it was picture of her from seconds earlier!

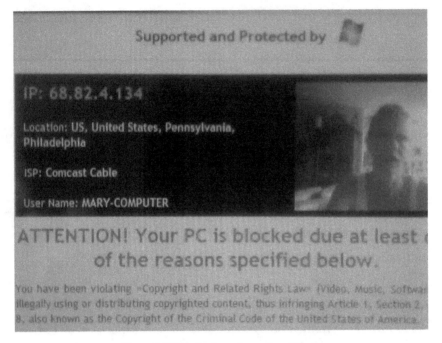

Photo 32. Mary's photo, from the affidavit.

A message also came up on the computer stating:

"You are facing 7–12 years in prison for illegally attempting to access copyrighted information."

She started yelling: "Charlie, they took my picture! They are threatening to put me in jail for 7–12 years."

That alone would be enough to scare most people into silence. But not the Stranges. Instead of being quiet, they called in their own troops: their lawyer Larry Klayman and channel 3, 6, and 10 news. All the news stations came to look at the computer.

Charlie, then remembered a computer expert from one of his men's retreats. David, who had several computer certifications, answered Charlie's call.

"What do you think David, can you fix it?" Charlie asked as he finished telling David the full story.

"Sure, Charlie. Let's try to remote access in and see what's going on," David said.

With no luck on remotely accessing the computer, Charlie asked David if he could drive it to him, about three hours away. So, Charlie and Mary drove south to Maryland to meet David and have him look at their computer.

After some time in the computer, David, more than surprised, said: "Oh my gosh, Charlie! What's in here they didn't even come out with yet!"

David proceeded to explain to Charlie that the viruses in his computer essentially destroyed it and they were viruses that he had never even seen before this. Eventually, David would make an official statement, which was presented during the NSA court case.

They had the testimony and evidence that the government was spying on them, but could they win in court?

The Lawsuit[10]

Larry Klayman, the Stranges' attorney and founder of Freedom Watch, filed suit in June 2013 at the U.S. District Court for the District of Columbia for "illegal seizure of phone records by the Obama administration's National Security Agency" naming Charlie and Mary as plaintiffs, and eventually converting it to a class action lawsuit.

The defendants named were President Barack Obama, Attorney General Eric Holder, the U.S. National Security Agency, NSA Director Keith B. Alexander, Verizon Communications, Verizon CEO Lowell C. McAdam, the U.S. Justice Department, and Roger Vinson, who was identified as a judge on the U.S. Foreign Intelligence Surveillance Court.

The complaint alleges constitutional violations including of the expectations of privacy, free speech, unreasonable searches and seizures, and due process.

The lawsuit claims that Charles and Mary were targeted in the NSA phone records scandal because of their criticism of Barack Obama's administration while they were pursuing the truth behind Extortion 17.

Underdogs

Charlie and Mary were the underdogs against the NSA—a middle-class couple from Philadelphia taking on the National Security Agency and the Obama administration.

But Michael had a special place in his heart for the underdog. From the times he saved someone's life on the street and in combat, no doubt Michael was rooting for Charlie and Mary from heaven. Michael wouldn't go looking for a fight, but he wouldn't back down when presented one.

When Michael was back in Philadelphia, there were two guys in a Wawa[21] parking lot beating up another guy. Onlookers just watched as the one man was being beaten to a pulp. As soon as Michael saw what was happening, he jumped into the fight and most likely saved the man's life, who needed an ambulance from the fight.

Once the cops showed up, bystanders explained Michael's role in helping the underdog, and Michael was able to swiftly leave and attend the party he was on his way to before he stopped at the Wawa.

Michael went in the backdoor of the party and didn't tell anyone what just happened; he just had a seat by the keg and went on with his night.

When others arrived at the party, they immediately recognized Michael and said, "You're the guy that just ended that fight in that Wawa parking lot!"

"Are you sure you have the right guy?" Michael humbly asked. He then smiled and went back to hanging out with friends.

Michael was sort of a superhero to his friends and family—helping

---

21   Wawa is a regional convenience store company.

the distraught laugh and smile, while at the same time not being afraid to stick up for others. When he joined the Navy, Michael became even more of a hero to his friends.

But unfortunately, Michael couldn't save everyone that he attempted to.

One tragedy that really shook Michael up was Adam Brown. Chief Petty Officer Adam Brown overcame demons such as drug addiction and jail to make it to the SEALs. Michael and Adam, friends, were on the same mission when Brown gave cover fire for his team and in the process was shot at close range.

Michael picked Brown up and with the team carried him a half-mile uphill. When Brown was laid down, the team realized that he had already passed. Adam Brown's heroic life story is told in the book *Fearless*.[11]

These stories help paint the picture of Michael, the SEAL Team 6 cryptologist who was considering becoming a nurse and/or firefighter after his military service. A caring and funny son, sibling, cousin, and uncle, and a fierce, intelligent warrior. Although it wasn't combat, fighting the NSA proved to be just as difficult. Charlie and Mary persevered and won the battle, but they are still fighting the war.

Court

That day in court, Charlie and Mary proudly walked in with Larry Klayman, as shown in Photo 33. They sat up front on one side, and the other side consisted of 14 lawyers for the Obama administration and the NSA. Edward Snowden's[22] lawyer was there for the court case, and Klayman talked to him for a few minutes before court began session.

---

22 Edward Snowden was a subcontractor for the National Security Agency who released documents demonstrating that the United States government was spying on its citizens. He escaped to Russia to protect himself from retaliation from the U.S. government. Was he a traitor or survivalist? What did he know about Extortion 17?

Photo 33: Charles (left), Larry Klayman (center), Mary Strange (right).

"Please rise, court is now in session, the Honorable Judge Leon is presiding. Please be seated."

Judge Richard J. Leon walked in wearing a bowtie as Charles, Mary, and the lawyers stood up and then sat down for the session.

Mr. James Gilligan, the NSA's lead lawyer started off the session, "Mr. Strange is a Gold Star Father, his son was an American hero, and we understand he's going through a lot of grief. But we do not spy on the American people here at the NSA. And we feel sorry for his loss."

Larry Klayman stood up and said, "Your Honor," as he's pulling out a newspaper, "it says right here in the Washington Post, 14 employees from the NSA fired for spying on their spouses," as he held up the newspaper.

Judge Leon glared at the lawyers for Obama and the NSA and slammed down the gavel and said, "This is my court, and you're going to lie to my face?! Can you find one time when you spied on an American citizen, and it stopped a terror attack here in America?"

And all 14 lawyers started to open up books, almost like a comedy show, flipping pages through quickly almost in sync with each other.

This wasn't the kind of comedy skit that Michael would impersonate. He loved quoting movies like Austin Powers or even making his own comedy skits from what seemed to be goofy commercials on local television ads or clips from the internet before the days of Google. Michael had a knack for comedy, but Judge Leon was very serious.

Judge Leon made them sweat for a few minutes.

And then Mr. Gilligan stood up and said, "No, Your Honor, we can't."

Judge Leon then said, "Do you know where you're at? You're in the third highest court in the United States, in Washington, DC.

"What you're doing to the Stranges is wrong. This is becoming an Orwellian State. Starting today, I want it to stop. I want you to stop spying and listening in on the Stranges."

That's when Klayman and the Stranges presented evidence (seen in Photo 34) of the text messages and the sworn statement from David.

Photo 34. Larry Klayman (center) speaking to Judge Leon with Dina James, Mary, and Charlie behind Klayman with James Gilligan, the head attorney for the Justice Department, standing on the right.

Ruling

The ruling made the headline with Photo 35 in the Philadelphia Inquirer: *Torresdale dad behind NSA lawsuit: "Every day, you feel sad"* and read:

Photo 35. Philadelphia Inquirer article regarding the NSA suit.

"The ruling in Washington by U.S. District Judge Richard J. Leon—who called the NSA data-collection program 'almost Orwellian' and ordered a halt that surely will be appealed all the way to the Supreme Court—is a landmark in the battle over how much the government can legally spy on its own citizens...

"But although Strange said it 'felt great' to learn of the judge's ruling in the suit he brought with well-known gadfly lawyer Larry Klayman of Freedom Watch, the NSA case isn't answering a question that still burns inside him: Exactly how and why was his son killed when the Chinook military helicopter carrying 30 U.S. servicemen and eight others was shot down west of Kabul on Aug. 6, 2011?"[12]

The Stranges beat the NSA twice, once in District Court and once in Circuit Court. When the case went to the Supreme Court, the law was changed. The Stranges would not win in the Supreme Court.

Charlie would continue to ask questions and stand up against the government until he and other Gold Star Parents of Extortion 17 were finally awarded with a hearing, Honoring the Heroes of Extortion 17, in Washington, DC.

CHAPTER 6
THE NATIONAL PRESS CLUB

"He has told you, O man, what is good; and what does the Lord require
of you but to do justice, and to love kindness,
and to walk humbly with your God?"
~Micah 6:8

IN 2013, CHARLES, WITH MARY behind him and Larry Klayman and other Extortion 17 parents by his side, spoke at the National Press Club. The following is a transcript of Charles' speech, edited for readability.

Charlie's Speech

Hello, everyone, my name is Charles Strange. My son's name was Michael Strange. Michael was a cryptologist for Special Operations; he was part of the Navy SEALs for SEAL Team Two for a few years, and the last almost four years, he was part of SEAL Team Six.

Michael was a brave American. He loved Philadelphia where we're from. He fought for this country. Michael being a crypto, the code for them is "Serve in Silence," And that silence was broken by our administration.

All of a sudden, there's movie SEAL Team Six, documentary SEAL

Team Six, SEAL Team Six, this this this? Where did it all start?

Joe Biden in Delaware, and a tuxedo with half a load on telling everybody, "It was the elite Navy SEAL Team."

And this is our Vice President.

Come on, man.

Michael knew what he was getting into. Michael knew what he was fighting for. Michael knew that someday he might have to give the ultimate sacrifice.

But not like this. To put my son in the most elite SEAL team in the world in a Chinook helicopter over an active battle that's going on for three and a half hours. Unacceptable. Unacceptable. Somebody must answer for this.

96 days after killing bin Laden? Suddenly, you're going to put 22 of the most elite SEAL Team Six in the world and eight other great Americans into a Chinook over a battle?

August 6, I got the call about my son's death. It's like a knife in my heart that turns every day. I cry every day. I get sad every day. Michael was 25 years old.

And we went to Dover to see the bodies. And we were all in the hanger down there when President Obama came up to me and he said "Mr. Strange," he grabs me by the shoulders, "Michael changed the way America lives."

I grabbed Mr. President by the shoulders, and I said, "I don't need to know about my son. I need to know what happened, Mr. President."

The Secret Service guys grabbed me. I'm crying. He went to give me a hug. And I whispered in his ear. I said, "Mr. President, is there going to be a congressional inquiry?"

And Mr. President whispered in my ear, and I could feel his lips touching, he said, Mr. Strange. "We're going to look into this very, very, very deep."

Well, I haven't heard anything.

October, we went down for General Colt's assessment of the investigation. When we got there, there was a projector screen, and other families there. General Colt was going over what happened.

He said it went through a chain of command for this landing site. I raised my hand, I said, "Sir, can I have the names of that chain of command?" His neck snaps.

He said, "it's in the book, sir."

I said, "how about the black box?"

The black box got blown away by the flood in Afghanistan. Come on. Can't find the black box, (which is really orange)?

I looked it up in Google, black boxes don't go away. They lose black boxes in the swamps in Florida, and they find them. You're going to tell me you can't find a black box? That's not acceptable. I tell my boss stuff like that, I get fired. Right?

My son, 25-year-old son, got set up and killed.

So, he [General Colt] goes on about "it's in the book. It's in the book." I have the book right here. They didn't put no ink in it. How can you give me a book with no ink in it?

I call up the command. They said, "we got a lot of complaints about that." I said, "send me another one."

"We burned it."

"You burned it?"

They gave us a disc. Put the disk in the computer. It's whited out. See two sentences. Whited out. My beautiful wife I'm looking at and I said, "we have to do something with this disc."

My wife's the genius, it's not me. Michael's stepmother, my heart and soul.

We printed it out. We print the disc out. It tells you everything.

It was a setup.

The Taliban sitting there with machine guns, motorcycles, phones. Who called them to tell them? It's right in the paperwork.

Karen mentioned it.

Billy mentioned it.

General Colt's asking questions. What happened to the air controller who was there to just check the area?

They're going into the Tangi Valley. The Tangi Valley it says in here is the "stronghold for the Taliban." You're going to put them in a Chinook over the stronghold of the Taliban? Did anybody check the area out?

Here it is right here. Everybody can get a copy. It says it's very brief. Again, "it's out of the task force," blank.

And it says something to the effect that "over 100 Taliban planned to travel from Providence through to Tangi Valley to possibly shoot down the coalition force."

May 11. 10 days after we killed bin Laden, the Taliban know who's coming in a Chinook helicopter.

Rules of Engagement.

It says in here. The Rangers are fighting the Taliban. They're chasing Qari Tahir. Eight of them. They kill six, two get away. Qari Tahir and his buddy run into 18 to 20. It's in the paperwork. They run into 18 to 20 of them. I said why didn't they take them out with a drone?

Admiral Harwood turns around and says, "to win the hearts and minds."

What about my heart? About my mind? I cry every day. My kids cry. To win hearts and minds, these people they hate us. They hate… my son told me they hate us.

They know the rules of engagement after the crash site. The Taliban walked up with kids in front of them to see if they could skin our kids alive. It's in the paperwork. I not making this up. I'm not military. It's in black and white pages.

So, this mission goes on. He asked about the air planners that were their planners in there. No, we didn't see them.

Who gave the okay?

Who is going to be held responsible? Someone has to be held responsible.

And it says in our paperwork. It goes all the way up to the top and mentions Petraeus and mentions Leon Panetta all the way to the top. So General Colt's given us this briefing. And he's telling us the helicopters coming in there won't go into it. It's pitch black, it's pitch black. But they see a couple guys on top of a building. They call up the Afghan administration to find out at two o'clock in the morning what these guys are doing on the building.

You know what they told them? They're hanging crops.

Now I'm from Philadelphia, and we don't have many crops there. But I don't know people that hang crops up at two o'clock in the morning. And this is supposedly where the shot came from. General Colt says they shot an RPG 150 to 200 yards in pitch dark with night vision goggles...

So, he says it's RPG is a lucky shot.

Are we playing basketball or hockey?

Is he out of his mind?

There's nothing lucky here. Our sons are dead! You know I raised my hand. I said, General Colt, it could have been a missile, a heat-seeking missile right, and there's no coincidence that he, Dougherty, and Woods might have found some heat-seeking missiles, MANPADs, 1000s. All of sudden you see what happened to them. All sudden all these SEAL Team Six guys are disappearing. Something is wrong.

We need a congressional inquiry. Somebody has to be accountable for the biggest loss in this war. There's no eye in the sky. They went off when the helicopter got shot down. It's in the paperwork. We didn't know what helicopter got shot. It took us 10 minutes.

My son Michael was fighting for his life. Nobody came in help. They didn't have the pathfinders there to check the area. Nobody checked the landing zone, nobody.

Who's calling the shots here? This is bullshit.

They told me my son had to be cremated. Everybody has to be cremated. My son didn't need to be cremated. I got pictures of my son! He was fighting. He had a gun in his hand. Come on. Fight for this country for us! And you're gonna lie to me, slap me in the face?

I called the command, I said why did you cremate my son? My son didn't want to be cremated. He's like, what do you mean? I got pictures of him. When I asked for the autopsy report from Dover. They sent me a disc with pictures. He's sitting there fighting.

"Everybody was burned beyond recognition." Everybody wasn't burned beyond recognition, another lie.

Somebody has to be held accountable. No pathfinders, all of a sudden the eye in the sky don't work. This is all fact. This is from the people that were there.

General Colt's statement in here, when he's questioning these guys, exact words: "Did a red flag go up when you put everybody in the same helicopter?"

No one knows the names of the Afghans they got on or not on the manifest. Something's wrong here.

I'm asking for the American people to help us for a change. Something has to be done.

"How did you assess the crash?"

"We had 30 plans to assess the crash. We had Blackhawks, we had pathfinders. We had 140 men going."

You knew it was going to crash?

You know? They knew just like the Taliban knew they're coming with 100 guys. They knew May 10. It's documented that SEAL Team Six was coming. Who's the leak?

Somebody has to be held accountable for it. And it's all black and white. It's fact. And who's profiting from this besides the Taliban and the al Qaeda? Huh? Follow the money.

And what happened in Benghazi. Somebody is leading something now. Something has to be done.

I'm asking everybody to stand up and please help us and I like to thank my friend here, Larry for standing up and leading us too with Billy and Karen.

That's all I got.

CHAPTER 7:
HONORING THE HEROES

"Do not gloat over me, my enemy! Though I have fallen, I will rise.
Though I sit in darkness, the LORD will be my light."
~Micah 7:8

25–30 TRIPS. THAT'S HOW MANY times the couple traveled from Philadelphia to Washington, DC, before a government official would consider helping the families of Extortion 17 ask questions in an official capacity. With Larry Klaymen, Ken Timmerman (one of the 66 hostages in the Iran hostage crisis), and multiple families from Extortion 17, the team went seeking representatives and senators, knocking on doors and asking for meetings seeking the truth.

When they finally found help in Representative Jason Chaffetz's office, they ended up with what the Stranges call a *horse and pony* show and the government called a congressional hearing.

Journeys to Washington, DC

Staying in nearby Alexandria, Virginia, at an affordable Best Western, the Stranges would meet other Extortion 17 families, Larry Klayman, and Ken Timmerman to seek out government officials—

representatives, senators, or anyone who might offer help in finding the truth of what happened to their sons and husbands.

Ken Timmerman is a best-selling author who has spent his career investigating the dark side of national security. He's interviewed dissidents behind the Iron Curtain, suicide bombers, and defectors of Iranian intelligence organizations and has covered multiple wars in the Middle East.[13] Ken wrote about Charlie's story in his book *Dark Forces: The Truth About What Happened in Benghazi*.

Throughout their journeys to Washington, DC, they met with Representatives Darrell Issa, Louie Gohmert, Michael Fitzpatrick, Michele Bachmann, Ileana Ros-Lehtinen, Trent Franks, John Carney, Walter Jones, Bob Brady, and Jason Chaffetz, and Senator Pat Toomey.

The Stranges appreciated each meeting, but no one was able to truly help, not even Chaffetz.[23] The saddest thing was that some had never heard of Extortion 17. Most listened and were sincerely sorry for their losses but were unable to help. Some would ask if the families needed a folder flag, but all they wanted were answers to a few questions.

The Stranges went to DC so many times searching for help and answers that they were recognized at the front gates, and security would alert each other, "the Stranges are here," telling who knows who that the couple was back in the building.

The group would knock on doors, would get a staffer, and be asked things like, "did you have an appointment?" "Can you come back at a different time?" They tried so hard for help but felt helpless.

Charlie thought, "We just need five minutes! Our sons died fighting for our country so you could be a representative or senator!" Realizing how sad it was when elected representatives couldn't or wouldn't do anything for the Gold Star group seeking answers was disappointing.

---

23   Chaffetz retired from Congress two days before Joni Marquez went public on Sean Hannity's show regarding her claims of falsehoods surrounding Extortion 17.

Securing a Hearing

In 2014, Larry Klaymen finally secured a hearing through the office of Jason Chaffetz, who sat on the Armed Services Committee. The Stranges were so excited, because they were going to finally be put in a position where they could ask relevant questions and expect realistic answers. But the hearing turned out to be just the opposite. Photo 36 shows the Stranges and others in Washington, DC, outside the hearing.

Photo 36. Charles and Mary Strange (center) in Washington, DC, before the hearing Honoring the Heroes.

Preparing Questions

In the beginning, the plan was that the parents and military would attend the hearing. Parents would ask prepared questions to the military about what happened. Some parents were also prepared to testify.

Forty-two parents wrote questions and submitted them in advance—they truly believed they were going to have a bona fide congressional hearing.

However, things quickly changed as the hearing became imminent. Three weeks prior, in Jason Chaffetz's office, James Lewis, Assistant Director of the Oversight Committee, alerted some participating families of unanticipated changes, starting with the Stranges.

Lewis said that all the parents could ask questions except for Mr. Strange.

Charlie started yelling as did Mary, and Klayman. They all felt frustrated and sad about the last-minute changes.

One of the parents set to testify received a call from an individual within the Central Intelligence Agency about his testimony before the hearing. Uncomfortable sharing details over the phone, he agreed to share specifics of his testimony in person in DC. However, shortly after that phone call, testimonies were no longer permitted at the hearing.

Now, all of the other parents were in the same situation as the Stranges: now none of parents could ask questions and there would be no parents testifying. They had to write their questions in advance and members of Congress would ask the questions.

Mary wrote a letter to those attending the hearing in a plea for the truth.

Mary's Letter

Dear Senators, Congress, and Members of The Armed Services Committee,

August 6, 2011, was the most devastating day in our lives. Every parent's worst nightmare, your child has been killed, along with 30 of his comrades in a foreign country. Imagine 30 families who on 08/05/2011 were strangers, 24 hours later, bonded forever.

My stepson, Michael Strange was on board the Chinook, call sign Extortion 17. Now, in our home, the loud laughter isn't as loud and holidays, family get-togethers, celebrations and just any "ordinary" day, there is that silent void that never goes away.

I have had to watch my husband cry every single day because his heart aches and he misses his son so much. Do you know what it's like, to watch the one person you love with all your heart, hurt so bad and know there's not a damn thing you can do?! I do, and it's a horrible feeling!

We have waited 30 months to be able to sit here today in the hope that this committee would help us find out what really happened that fateful night.

Personally, I feel as if salt has been added to the wound by not allowing any parents to speak here today. My husband and I have spent many sleepless nights, shed many tears, and spent thousands of hours reading, researching, making calls, and doing a whole lot of good ol' fashioned footwork knocking on doors trying to get some answers. In response, we have been lied to, treated disrespectfully, and talked to as if we were morons. It's disgraceful! I can't believe this is what Gold Star Parents have to tolerate!

There have been sooo many inconsistencies in the reports and stories for this to be "a lucky shot." So, please do not insult us with an outrageous and offensive excuse as that!!

Let's begin with Colt's statement in his "Summary" of what happened. He states that the "CH-47D Air Mission Commander and his task force commander determined this mission to be a 'high-risk mission' due to the experience level of one non-pilot crew chief and because of this high risk, the mission had to be approved by The Higher Headquarters Commander for Special Operations Task Force and the Supporting Aviation Brigadier Commander." Who are these incompetent individuals?

Why would they OK all 30 men on 1 CH-47, if before leaving the forward operating base (FOB), it was determined to already be a high-risk mission? Then, they gave no escorts for Extortion 17 on an already high-risk mission into a hot landing zone (HLZ)?

Standard Operating Procedures (SOP) were not followed because they should have had an escort (AC-130 Gunship OR an AH-64 Apache) upon leaving the FOB [Forward Operating Base]! Our men had none!

General Colt states, "the Ranger-led assault force was supported by 2 CH-47D Chinook helicopters and 2 AH-64 Apache attack helicopters, along with an AC-130 Gunship, and a relatively robust team of intelligence, surveillance, and reconnaissance (ISR) aircraft."

Then, to add insult to injury, the next line is as follows "The 2 CH-47Ds would airlift the Assault Force, totaling 47 personnel, into a landing zone approximately 1200 meters from the suspected location, of the Tangi Valley Taliban Leader, Qari Tahir a.k.a. OBJECTIVE LEFTY GROVE."

So, there were 47 Rangers and 31 Americans aboard Extortion 17, that equals 78 of our Special Operators to CAPTURE 1 Taliban Leader??!! Why?

Then, when the Rangers arrived at their target compound, "Overhead Manned and Unmanned Aircraft observed several personnel departing the target area. The AH-64 Apache attack helicopters detected and positively identified suspected Taliban fighters armed with AK-47 rifles and "RPG" launchers, walking single file approximately 400 meters northwest of the target compound."

"Throughout the execution of the mission the Overhead ISR aircraft continued to track the movement of suspected Taliban fighters. This group formed around two personnel who were observed moving northwest from the immediate vicinity of the target area, before the

Ranger-led assault force had arrived." Did they know the Rangers were coming? Sure sounds like it to me!

"There were Taliban in the trees, on motorcycles, in the building, approx. 2 kilometers from the original compound." They knew all this, but still allowed our boys to go in a HLZ, all 31 Americans on one helicopter?

We were told the Rangers needed help because they were under attack. Then, we come to find out...are you ready for this...the Rangers were never in danger!

Our boys did not have to be deployed that night as an IRF [Immediate Response Force]. So, why were they?

The 7 Afghan Commandos who originally on Extortion 17 either got off and refused to get back on or were switched out and 7 new Afghans got on. Who were they? Why were they never questioned? Who made these decisions? How come General Colt never asked these questions? Are the 7 that aborted Extortion 17 still being allowed to fly with our Special Operators? If so, why?

In the "Investigation Paperwork" "Exhibit 89" [Appendix E] Colt asks the Air Force Commander (AFC) "What is the assessment of the Tangi Valley?" AFC answers "over 100 Taliban plan to travel from the [redacted] Province to the Tangi Valley to shoot down the Coalition Force Aircraft." They knew and did nothing to prevent this?! WHY when our Men Requested Pre-Assault Fire 2–3 times, to clear the hot landing zone they were denied! Who denied that request?

The Occupational Coordination Group (OCG) has the final say in every mission our Special Operations does, whether it is a go or if they don't like it, they can call the mission off!

"How the hell can we ever win a war, when the enemy knows all of our moves before we do them?!

Where are the black boxes?

On Oct.12, 2011 General Colt, when my husband (Charles Strange) asks this question, Colt replies "A flash flood came and washed it away!"

We have looked into this, and those boxes don't go away, in fact they have beacons on them and can be found 20,000 feet underwater! So, we ask again, where are the black boxes? What don't they want us to hear on those recordings?

There were 3 "eyes in the sky," But, not one on Extortion 17. Why? General Colt asks about them and is told "We never did a mission like this, Sir [Colt]. It made us feel VERY vulnerable. Our hands were tied from up above." How far up is "UP ABOVE?" WHO gave this command? 95 days prior ALL EYES were on SEAL Team 6 from the Situation Room.

My stepson, CTR1 Michael Strange, was cremated. He did not need to be! Why were we told, "They are all burned beyond recognition," "no identifiable remains," and "only 38 C-Spines and skulls left."? Lies, lies, and more lies! Why?

We need help finding the truth! Why are the parents and loved ones of Extortion 17 being allowed to be treated this way? The men of Extortion 17 were men of courage, integrity, and honor. Not only did the families lose their loved ones but this country lost 30 heroic defenders of freedom.

Please help the Families of Extortion 17 find some closure and that can only begin with the Truth. We deserve that much!

The only time you have to lie is if you know what you're doing is wrong.

-Maryann Strange

The Hearing Honoring the Heroes

Representative Jason Chaffetz, chairman of the House Oversight and Government Reform Subcommittee on National Security facilitated the hearing. The panel consisted of members representing the Pentagon[24]: Garry P. Reid, the special operations and low-intensity conflict advisor at the U.S. Department of Defense (DoD); Colonel John Devillier, commander of Air Force Operations at the U.S. DoD; Kirk Brown, director of Army Casualty and Mortuary Affairs Operations Center at the U.S. DoD; and Aaron Brodsky, director of Naval Casualty Services at the U.S. DoD. The hearing was broadcast on CSPAN-3.

Opening Statements

Jason Chaffetz opened the hearing: "This hearing, Afghanistan, Honoring the Heroes of Extortion 17, has been extraordinarily difficult to organize [...] because it's proved nearly impossible to effectively solicit and subsequently meet the needs and wishes of every family member or loved one that was on board Extortion 1-7.

"I want to assure the families that this committee **questioned the Department of Defense officials on the full spectrum of the mission,** to include extremely sensitive and highly classified information, in an effort to fully understand the events pertaining to the strategy that unfolded that day.

"We have tried our best to treat all families' interests equally… Some families may claim we have not done enough by not allowing classified or highly graphic information to be discussed today… **There are things that we cannot and will not be discussing…**"

Charlie knew, almost right away, that this wasn't going to be a real

---

24 The majority of the panel weren't in their positions when Extortion 17 happened.

hearing—he wasn't permitted to ask questions. The families weren't permitted to ask questions. No families could testify. Chaffetz had stated that the committee had already questioned the Department of Defense on the full spectrum of the mission.

Casualty Assistance

Since most of the panel was from some form of a casualty operations office, most of the questions were naturally related to the treatment of the brave fallen heroes' bodies: questions regarding policies and procedures related to ceremonies, travel, placement of flags on coffins, and other similar questions about fallen heroes and casualties. *Note: these questions were all pertinent to the respectful treatment of fallen heroes, but neglected questions related to the actual shootdown of the Chinook.*

One of the specific questions the Stranges had was around the treatment of Michael's body, which was "too gruesome" to discuss at the hearing. Again, Michael's parents were told that he was burned to death therefore he was cremated, only for Charlie to find out from the Dover autopsy report that his son wasn't burned beyond recognition at all—his body was intact.

Mission Questions

Representative John Mica of Florida asked the most mission-related questions directly to Garry Reid. In Charlie's opinion, Mica was the only one who had read the questions from the Gold Star Parents.

"We put our men in equipment that couldn't be protected. Why would we risk a high-risk mission on putting our men on this kind of equipment (a Chinook)?" asked Mica.

"Who was in charge of the mission, the individual? We need to be hearing from that individual." Mica said directly to Reid.

"What Afghans had information on this mission?" Mica pressed on Reid again.

These questions weren't answered.

Charlie's Thoughts

Charlie at first wondered why they were calling it "Honoring the Heroes of Extortion 17," with nothing noting an investigation into the events of the call sign Extortion 17 shootdown. Although he was grateful for the committee honoring the heroes, the hearing didn't answer basic questions like:

- Why weren't any Afghans interviewed?

- Who oversaw the mission?

- What was the result of the Department of Defense questioning that wasn't permitted to be a part of the hearing?

The relentless Charles Strange didn't stop at the hearing, Honoring the Heroes, and found his way into the Pentagon to question Garry Reid face-to-face.

CHAPTER 8:
THE PENTAGON

"We are from God, and whoever knows God listens to us;
but whoever is not from God does not listen to us. This is how we
recognize the Spirit of truth and the spirit of falsehood."
~ 1 John 4:6

AFTER MULTIPLE ATTEMPTS, REPRESENTATIVE BOB Brady was able to help the Stranges possibly get some answers to the questions surrounding Michael's death. Brady, from Philadelphia, knew of Michael and his missions. He knew Charlie was a part of the labor union. The first meeting with Representative Brady was in 2012 at his office in Washington, DC, without success. However, after the hearing, Brady was able to get the Stranges into the Pentagon to meet directly with Garry Reid.

Representative Brady in 2012

"Representative Brady, help me, help me please…" Charlie begged.

"They were set up, you know it!" Charlie began to shout.

Representative Brady's security outfit summoned the police.

"There's no need to call the police," Representative Brady, shown in Photo 37, stated. He knew Michael's role in the bin Laden raid and respected both Michael and Charles.

But, Brady didn't know how to help Charles, and nothing more happened until 2014, after the hearing.

Photo 37. Representative Brady and Charles after the 2012 meeting, when Brady requested a photo with Charles.

Getting the Meeting

In 2014, after the hearing, Brady was able to get the couple into the Pentagon to ask Garry Reid questions face-to-face.

For this meeting with Garry Reid, they weren't permitted any other parents, lawyers, or news.

And, the Pentagon wanted them to send the send questions in advance, which they did, and which the Pentagon "did not receive."

The Pentagon requested that the Stranges not tell anyone they were coming—so they told everyone, including radio and TV stations in Philadelphia.

Questioning Garry Reid

In Spring 2014, the Stranges pulled into the Pentagon parking lot and were met with two officers with machine guns who drove them toward an office. Charles and Mary met with Garry Reid, David Steindl, Natalia Henriquez, and Joe Martin.

"Hi Mr. Strange, thanks for coming. I know you have some questions for us."

"Yes, Garry, Extortion 17 was a complete setup. The Taliban knew they were coming. We want to know what happened."

"Well, Charlie, you can't believe everything you read on the internet," Garry Reid said to Charlie about Extortion 17 being a setup.

Charlie, asked: "Did you even read the 1364 pages? Did you even look at them?" Charlie was both surprised and angry Reid wouldn't read the 1364 pages about the largest loss of life in Afghanistan where 30 Americans died.

"We read the summary report from General Colt, yes." Reid responded.

"Are you kidding me? You brought us all the way to the Pentagon, and you didn't even read the 1364 pages? Is this a joke?"

Charlie slammed down Exhibit 89 [Appendix E] that stated the Taliban were prepared to shoot down a coalition aircraft a few days after the bin Laden raid—a statement that contradicted Reid's statements at the hearing.

"Where did you get this?!" asked Reid as they all looked down at the paper and back up at Charlie.

"It's in the 1364 pages! Why didn't you read them? You didn't even prepare for our meeting after all this time and effort!"

Charlie shouted again: "Were you too busy with Chuck Hagel planning another fundraiser?"

The security guards took Charlie outside.

When he came back in, Mary had already assumed Charlie's position and was yelling at Garry Reid and the others about the information in the pages—how the Taliban was on the roof, passing objects back and forth—presumably RPGs or MANPADs—as the families were told it was someone hanging crops.

Mary showed Reid another excerpt which reinforced that Extortion 17 was a setup.

Garry Reid stood strong on his position.

Mary shouted again, pointing her finger at Garry Reid: "Why were there seven Afghans on board with the most elite unit in the world and you don't even know the names?!"

Reid gave a completely different answer than they heard at the hearing—insinuating to the Stranges that Reid was not telling the truth and hiding important information.

"You're a bad person!" Mary shouted. "You're a stone-cold liar."

She continued shouting and screaming at Reid as it was Charlie's turn to calm her down. He pulled her away as she was pointing her finger at Reid yelling about his lies and deceit.

After about 45 minutes of accomplishing very little with Garry Reid, Charles left 10–12 pages from the 1364 at the Pentagon along with a list of questions, hoping for follow-up. On the way out of the Pentagon, Reid followed them out and commented that his son was in college at Villanova.[25] Charlie felt the twist of a dagger in his heart, giving him a painful reminder of Michael.

Follow-Up

After some time, Charlie called the liaison about the status of the answers to the questions. The liaison stated they had lost the questions. So, Charlie called Bob Brady, who was furious at the Pentagon and sent the questions again.

To this day, Charlie has never heard back from the Pentagon regarding answers to his questions.

Following that meeting, Charlies and Mary sent the following letter to Natalia Henriquez, Dan Davis, and Joseph Martin from the White House and Navy on May 2, 2014:

> "We would like to first say Thank You to Representative Bob Brady and his staff, for arranging a meeting at the Pentagon for me, my wife, and certain members of the Military to sit and ask the many unanswered questions regarding the death of 30 Brave Warriors on 08/06/2011 on a helo [helicopter], call sign, Extortion 17.
> "My Son, Michael Strange was on board that helicopter. This was the biggest loss in a single incident in both Iraq and Afghanistan, 30 Brave Americans were killed. It was the biggest loss EVER to our Special Ops, onboard were 22 Special Operators and some of those were from the Elite DEVGRU group.
> "On April 30, 2014, we [Charlie and Mary] drove to the Pentagon in Arlington, VA, to meet with Garry Reid, Rear Admiral David Steindl, LCDR Natalia Henriquez, and Joe

---

25 Billy and Karen Vaughn have a similar story about Admiral McRaven picking his daughter up at the airport from college.

Martin, so we could ask some of the questions we have
been asking for the last 32 months and hopefully get some
answers. We found it SO disheartening to learn that NOT
one of the four even read the 1364 pages from Brig. General Jeffrey Colt's "investigation" into the deaths of these 30
men, BUT Mr. Reid DID let us know that he read Billy
Vaughn's book 'Betrayal.'

"How can you give an argument when you DON'T have
all the facts?? Both Mary and I were stunned! I know it
wasn't their sons in that crash, but a little respect would
have been nice! I have to say that Mr. Reid did read the
summary of the sketchy "investigation" and he watched
our National Press Club video, so for that we are grateful.

"Also, we appreciate the honesty of saying 'I don't know'
instead of trying to give us some BS answer! Yes, in a couple areas we were given a perspective we had not thought
of before since we're not military. We would like to meet
again with this group, AFTER they take the time to read
the 1364 pages, especially Exhibits 42, 43, 47, 62, 63 & 89
[Appendices E–J].

"On behalf of the ALL the Gold Star Parents of Extortion
17, we're requesting a NEW investigation into what happened to our sons. We have since the beginning been lied
to over and over again...WHY? There are more questions
than answers that General Colt just NEVER pursued in his
'investigation.'

"It is not only us Parents asking, but the American people
want to know what happened. We deserve to know the
circumstances of how our Sons REALLY died!! WE WILL
NOT STOP OR GO AWAY UNTIL WE FEEL SATIS-

FIED WITH THE ANSWERS WE GET!!! We feel the only way to do that is through a 'NEW Investigation,' a thorough investigation!

"My wife, Mary, gave Mr. Reid an outline of what we want included in the investigation. If you have any questions, please feel free to contact us. Thank You again for your time.

Sincerely,

Charles and Mary Ann Strange

A Call to Action

Two months after Charlie and Mary sent the letter, they followed up with the Pentagon. The Pentagon stated they lost the questions.

All the Stranges and other families have asked for is a bona fide congressional hearing to ask some of the obvious questions regarding the downing of call sign Extortion 17 and the deaths of their sons.

Charles Strange remembers the words of his son Michael two months before the crash: **"Dad, you'll never believe what's happening in this country."** After the shootdown, Charles has questioned the official narrative—questioning Barack Obama in Dover and asking for a congressional hearing.

During the formal debrief and the paperwork provided afterwards, Charles was exposed to a different narrative conflicting with the official summary investigation. The Stranges conclusion of Extortion 17 being set up is all from official government documents, the 1364 pages. These pages painted a story of potential cover-up and insider involvement surrounding the largest loss of American life in the War on Terror. And, according to the paperwork, it goes all the way to the top.

During the Honoring the Heroes of Extortion 17 hearing,

Representative John Mica asked who oversaw the mission—a question that was never answered.

In the official 1364 pages, one person interviewed said the mission made them feel vulnerable and their hands were tied from above. But from who and why?

The families of Extortion 17, including the Stranges, and the American people deserve the truth.

CHAPTER 9:
GOLD STAR DAD

"They must turn from evil and do good;
they must seek peace and pursue it."
~1 Peter 3:11

IT'S DIFFICULT TO FIND PEACE when evidence suggests Michael and the other men may have been betrayed by someone in the same country he defended to his death. It's even more difficult to find peace when every year, Memorial Day, Michael's birthday, and Independence Day seem to be back-to-back-to-back over three long months.

Charlie won't have complete peace until justice is served, but he does find some peace through healing and comforting other Gold Star Families through the Michael Strange Foundation. The foundation has been helping Gold Star Families, especially from the Global War on Terror, since 2012.

The support for the Michael Strange Foundation is immense. The foundation has touched hundreds of lives directly through the Weekend Workshops. And, thanks to strong supporters, thousands more know about the foundation and its work to help Gold Star Families.

The White House

In June 2017, President Trump invited Charlie and Mary to the White House along with nine other Gold Star Parents.[14] At one point, they were alone with President Trump and the First Lady for about fifteen minutes.

Charlie didn't waste any time at all before discussing Extortion 17.

"I'm a little nervous to talk to you, Mr. President, do you mind if I pull out my notes?" Charles asked.

President Trump looked toward the Secret Service member near him, turned and smiled and looked at Charlie and said "Sure, Mr. Strange" as he continued smiling at Charlie.

Charlie pulled out his reader glasses and two pages of the 1364 pages preparing to talk to President Trump.

Charlie began reading from the 1364 pages, detailing that call sign Extortion 17 was a setup and that the investigation done by Colt wasn't a real investigation. He started to show Trump the evidence in the pages, how the Taliban was traveling to the Tangi Valley to shoot down coalition forces just after the bin Laden raid.

Trump started reading the pages, looking at Charlie and back to the pages.

"Can I keep these, Mr. Strange?"

"Absolutely," stated Charlie.

Trump then handed the pages to the Secret Service member present and stated, "Take these, and make sure I get Mr. Strange's notes tonight, so I can read them over!"

At the end of the conversation, both President and First Lady Trump gave Charlie a hug.

"I can't believe what you're going through. And I have a son of my own. I can't even imagine it, we're so sorry," said First Lady Melania.

Charlie thanked them and the two couples took a photo together, shown in Photo 38.

Photo 38. Charles and Mary with President and First Lady Trump at the White House

That Christmas, The White House asked the Stranges to a Christmas dinner at the White House. Charles and Mary had the opportunity again to meet with President and First Lady Trump, as seen in Photo 39.

Photo 39. Charles Strange, First Lady Melania Trump, President Trump,
Mary Ann Strange

Charlie's Healing

After Michael's death, Charlie was asked to be a guest speaker about the effects of war. At first, Charlie was upset when Gene McMahon called him and asked him to come to a Vets Journey Home[26] meeting, speak, and participate.

"Why the hell would I want to come when my son didn't make it home? What's wrong with you?" Charlie replied to McMahon's guest-speaking request.

Charlie was extremely reluctant to sit around with veterans who made it back home as it would cause too much pain. But when McMahon called back again after some time had passed, Charlie reluctantly agreed to speak, hoping he could bring some peace to others. But he ended up finding some peace himself.

Charlie not only spoke at a Vets Journey Home meeting, he also participated and learned how to help facilitate healing. Many of the soldiers he spoke to suffered from post-traumatic stress disorder (PTSD), and during an exercise, they all stated what was bothering them. Many of the men and women discussed anger, sex, drinking, divorce, and other negative impacts on their life, all due to effects of war.

And when they asked Charlie: "What's bothering you?" Charlie answered, "Well, I got a piece of my heart missing," referring to the death of Michael in Afghanistan.

That's when the healing began. They laid Charlie across a few chairs and formed a circle around him, playing meditation-type music. Then each person took a turn, standing over him. They touched their heart and touched Charlie's heart and said, "here's a piece of my heart," giv-

---

26 Vets Journey Home is an organization dedicated to helping veterans with emotional issues from their time in military service. More information at www.vetsjourneyhome.com.

ing Charlie a metaphorical piece of their heart to help him find some peace and comfort.

Charlie started crying, thinking about Michael, and the entire experience was extremely emotional. Charlie got a bit of healing and felt a little bit better after that weekend. He realized that he needed to help other Gold Star Families—especially parents—find peace through healing. And that's how the Michael Strange Foundation started.

The Michael Strange Foundation

The Stranges started the Michael Strange Foundation in 2012 with help from Charlie's friend Michael Quinn. The foundation is a non-profit organization, set up in Michael's memory, focusing on healing Gold Star Families. Its mission is to provide unconditional support and services to the families of recently fallen service members by professionals in several fields and by those who have suffered similar losses so that the healing process can begin.

In Charlie and Mary's opinion, there is an overwhelming outpouring of support initially, but it is the following months that are the most difficult when the ceremonies fade away and there is a lack of people who truly understand what it means to suffer such a devastating and traumatic loss.

For Gold Star Families, much of the support dwindles after time as people get back to their lives, but for a Gold Star, their life will never be the same. Charlie understands this, which is one of the reasons the foundation has Weekend Workshops—an all-expense paid weekend for Gold Stars to get together for comradery, remembrance, and healing.

Weekend Workshops

The first Weekend Workshop took place near Philadelphia at Malvern Retreat House with 15 Gold Star Parents. The second weekend took place in Ocean City, Maryland, with 42 Gold Star Parents. Charlie has held 10 Gold Star weekends at locations ranging from Philadelphia to DC, Colorado, Arizona, Massachusetts, and New Jersey. Hundreds of Gold Star Parents have participated in the Michael Strange Foundation Weekend Workshops.

One of the weekends for Extortion 17 Gold Star Families was in Washington, Massachusetts, where Eyal Shapira, president of the Raritan Central Railway, coordinated a memorial for Extortion 17 heroes as shown in Photo 40 and 41.[15] Many of the families of Extortion 17 got together at the memorial.

Photo 40. Extortion 17 memorial in Lenox, MA, with some family members present.

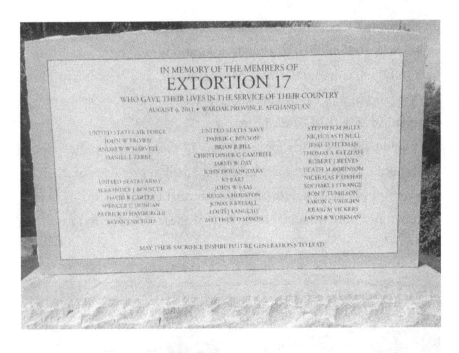

Photo 41. Extortion 17 memorial in Lenox, MA.

Charlie, Mary, and others continue to build on each Weekend Workshop, making the experience as healing as possible. Every Weekend Workshop starts with the Pledge of Allegiance, National Anthem, and prayer. The Gold Star Families are very patriotic, just as their sons and daughters were.

"This is not a group we filled out an application for," says Mike Anderson, a Gold Star Father, who lost his son Marine Cpl. Michael Anderson in Iraq in 2004. "We paid our dues with the blood of our children. We didn't want to join, but we have a lifetime membership."[16]

During the workshops, all Gold Stars gather near an American flag, and each set of parents introduces themselves at the podium: where they are from, who their son or daughter is, and just friendly information about their lives and loved one they lost. The newly acquainted parents begin to bond with each other, some starting relationships that will last a lifetime.

Parents write a letter to their loved one on Friday evening. On Saturday morning, with the grief counselor present, parents place photos of their lost sons and daughters on an honorary table, as shown in Photo 42.

Photo 42. Honorary table at the Michael Strange Foundation Weekend Workshop.

The Stranges, with the grief counselor, then discuss the stages of grief with hope that the weekend and relationships formed will help parents in all stages move toward *acceptance and hope.*

The parents read their letter out loud to their son or daughter. This is an extremely emotional experience, and many are, at first, reluctant to share such a moment in a group setting, but many if not all find the experience both rewarding and relieving. One group of Gold Star Parents is seen in Photo 43 with photos of their sons and daughters.

Photo 43. Gold Star Parents holding photos of their sons and daughters during a Gold Star Workshop in Ocean City, MD.

The foundation brings in guest speakers like Patrick Mudge, chief executive officer of Icey-Tek USA LLC. Patrick's story is one of struggle with PTSD, nearly attempting suicide, recovering, and healing to become a successful businessman. Speakers like Mudge help Gold Star Parents further overcome grief and sadness through such personal, emotional stories about the negative impacts of war.

The foundation has also hosted other speakers like Rob O'Neill and Drago. Rob O'Neill has donated his time for two Weekend Workshops to help Gold Star Families. Drago and his wife from the Navy SEALs Fund have been such a great asset to helping Gold Star Families, the Michael Strange Foundation, and the brotherhood.

During the Weekend Workshops and other events throughout the weekend involving the public, Gold Star Parents like Collie Tomlinson and Steve and Donna Fowlkes shown in Photos 44 and 45 also speak to crowds that gather to show support for the foundation and Gold Star Families.

Photo 44. Charlie (speaking, left) and Collie Tomlinson, right.

Photo 45. Steve Fowlkes (speaking) with his wife Donna,
and Charlie behind him. Mary Strange on the right.

Gold Stars are often escorted by biker groups such as the Punishers, Warriors' Watch, and others from location to location giving them some of the special treatment that they deserve. Photos and videos for the foundation are taken by Bob and Millie Hilgrube, who have been volunteering at every weekend since the second workshop in Ocean City, MD.

Support for the Foundation

Support for the Michael Strange Foundation is strong and is increasing as Charlie, Mary, and other foundation supporters invite more Gold Star Families and get the word out about the Weekend Workshops.

When in Philadelphia, parents are invited to bring memorabilia and photos to Tony Luke's,[17] a sandwich shop owned by Papa Tony Lucidonio Senior and son, Nicky Lucidonio. The Lucidonios support the Michael Strange Foundation by donating meals and money, and, most importantly, allowing Gold Star Families to bring photos and memorabilia of their lost loved one and place them inside the Michael Strange Foundation wall, pictured in Photo 46.

Photo 46. Nicky Lucidonio in front of the Michael Strange Foundation wall at Tony Luke's in Philadelphia, PA.

Bill Colfer of Specialty Freight Services honored and remembered Michael and other Gold Star Families by placing a mural of Michael, the Michael Strange Foundation, and its mission on his trucks, shown in Photo 47 and 48. Colfer donates regularly to the Michael Strange Foundation.

Photo 47. Photo of Bill Colfer with the Michael Strange Foundation truck.

Photo 48. Charles standing next to the Michael Strange Foundation truck owned by Bill Colfer.

Vision

The Stranges' work never ends. They spend time speaking at events, for Extortion 17 and the foundation, live and on shows like Live Truth Radio with Brian Lange. Charlie is in constant communication with Gold Star Parents and is facilitating the creation of new relationships among Gold Stars to further spread hope and peace.

Their vision is to continue Gold Star weekends more frequently, with a house on the beach to accommodate intimate gatherings, yet hopefully with a growing number of Gold Star Families in attendance.

He and Mary aim to reach each of the 7,000 lost warriors' parents in the Global War of Terror. Additionally, he and others involved with the foundation wish to have different levels of healing and continue to invite back Gold Stars who have already participated for further ongoing healing.

The weekends are truly unlike anything else available for Gold Star Families—facilitated by Gold Star Families and friends in an intimate setting with a mix of guest speakers, healing exercises, role playing, and relationship building.

The foundation won the Humanitarian Award from the Four Chaplains, shown in Photo 49, and was featured in a number of newspapers for its work with Gold Star Families. As Mike Anderson told People Magazine regarding the Weekend Workshops: "We laughed, we cried, we broke bread, we bonded."[18]

Photo 49. Award from Four Chaplains.

Donations to the foundation go toward expenses, which include travel, means, and hotels, associated with Weekend Workshops and similar events for Gold Star Families. For more information or to donate to the Michael Strange Foundation, please visit PO1Strange.org.

Afterword
By Charles Strange

Yea, though I walk through the valley of the shadow of death, I will fear no evil: for thou art with me; thy rod and thy staff they comfort me.
~Psalm 23:4

AUGUST 6, 2011. THE DAY that changed my life forever. There's a knife in my heart every day. And I will walk with a limp for the rest of my life. Michael was prepared to make the ultimate sacrifice, but not like this. Not in a setup involving the people he trusted.

Extortion 17

Extortion means the unlawful demanding and obtaining of something (silence) through force. Why was this Chinook's call sign Extortion 17?

In 2008, the Battle of Wanat in Afghanistan, nine soldiers died. In this case, Central Command did an exhaustive 18-month investigation, under pressure from one senator and family members into what happened, much, much more thorough than Extortion 17's investigation.

Guess what they found? Complicity in the Taliban attack by the local Afghan government in that province and by the Afghanistan

National Army. Why can't an investigation like this be done? Why won't they investigate Extortion 17?

I knew something was wrong on June 4, 2011, two months before he was killed. While everyone else was celebrating the death of bin Laden, Michael was tormented. Michael should have been celebrating his 25th birthday on June 6, 2011, but instead was talking about a will to his family and friends. He said to me, "Dad, you'll never believe what's happening in this country."

I've spoken to other parents whose children were on the bin Laden raid—many of them were also tormented when they came home. Many gave signs that something was wrong. But no one really knows for *what* and *why*.

For a country the size of Texas, Afghanistan has brought significant hurt to the United States in many forms. For the top military in the world to be fighting in the country the size of Texas should give anyone a signal that something is wrong.

Over 7,000 men and women have died in Iraq and Afghanistan, resulting in over 14,000 Gold Star Parents grieving. Plus, their grandparents, siblings, friends, neighbors, cousins, and teammates. The loss of one person has a ripple effect on our communities and impacts millions of people.

Over 30,000 men and women who have returned from Iraq and Afghanistan have killed themselves. Over 500,000 have been directly impacted by opium and heroin. Essentially, all Americans have been impacted in some way or another from Afghanistan. Follow the money.

In the case of Extortion 17, I am implicating bad actors in the United States, bad individuals. I'm not saying that the U.S. military or the U.S. government killed my son. But, I do believe that bad actors within the United States coordinated with other bad actors in the Taliban and maybe Karzai, the former president of Afghanistan, to shootdown Extortion 17.

Remember, Karzai was the first one to say it was SEAL Team 6. How did he know? And I believe it's got something to do with bin Laden and the pallets of money sent to Iran.

I tried to get Michael out of the SEALs early. Michael wanted to be there, and he was good at what he did. Everyone wants to be on SEAL Team 6. The status, prestige, and pay that come with it are second to none within the military.

Michael started working out and eating differently, preparing to go into the Navy. We would run the Rocky steps together for him to work out. Michael learned some Arabic and Pashto. His team stopped terrorist attacks within the United States. Michael was indeed a hero.

You may not understand the magnitude of all the questions, like *who were the Afghans onboard the Chinook*. But there were over 300 of our soldiers killed in green-on-blue attacks. This is where the Afghan soldiers who were trained by the United States actually attacked and killed our servicemen and women. That's why it's so important to know who the Afghans on the helicopter were, why they were switched out, and who was in charge of the manifest. That's just one of our many questions.

When President Obama told me he was going to look into this *very, very, very deep*, I never realized at the time how deep it actually goes. But, after August 6, 2011, more admirals and generals left or retired in that month of August than in the history of America. Why? After the investigation, Brigadier General Jeffery Colt was promoted to Major General, just like the guy who did the investigation on Pat Tillman[27] was promoted.

There were six IEDs at the landing site and IEDs going to the landing site. At the moment that Extortion 17 went down, all three eyes in the sky went out. Coincidence.

---

27   Pat Tillman was an NFL football player on the Arizona Cardinals who gave up his career to go and fight for his country after 9-11.

The Tangi Valley is known to be a bright valley with firepits at nighttime, but on August 6, 2011, there was no fires at all in the Tangi Valley. Another coincidence. I believe this means everyone, even the locals, knew SEAL Team 6 and the Chinook were coming to the valley. They were prepared.

The night vision goggles (NVG) worked for the Taliban that night, but not our soldiers. All eyes were on SEAL Team 6 three months earlier during the bin Laden raid in the Situation Room. Now, 96 days later, no one was watching SEAL Team 6 on Extortion 17: all three eyes in the sky went out simultaneously. More coincidences?

Before the election in 2020, news hit the media that Biden didn't reveal the names of the SEAL Team 6 members on the bin Laden raid. But he didn't have to. He did say that the SEAL Team got bin Laden. Why would he do this?

This is the first time in the history of America that a team was given public acknowledgment. No one had ever attributed any mission directly to the SEALs. Robert Gates, the secretary of defense, was upset about this. Biden didn't have to release their exact names to put a target on their backs. And that's exactly what he did. But why? More coincidences?

It's been ten years, why are things still classified? If the war is over, why are things still classified? Why wouldn't Chaffetz allow any mission-related questions at the Honoring the Heroes Hearing? Why did Chaffetz leave the government almost at the exact same time that Joni Marquez became a whistleblower for the victims of Extortion 17? Why didn't anyone including Gary Reid read the full 1364 pages, but only the 25-page summary report? There are too many coincidences. There are more questions than answers. The evidence is mounting that someone at the top is responsible for the downing of Extortion 17.

Michael Strange Foundation

Through my foundation work with Gold Stars, I've learned that the military always sends a CACO that had never knocked on a door of a new Gold Star. They never had to tell parents about losing their child before. That's why they never know what to do or what to say. That way they aren't giving away any additional information.

Our Gold Stars need more support. Once the truth of Extortion 17 becomes public, and the malice behind the scenes in Afghanistan becomes common knowledge, our great Gold Stars will need even more comforting. And that's where the Michael Strange Foundation will come to their assistance.

Appendix A

THEY SERVED IN SILENCE

The Story of a Cryptologic Hero
CTR1 Michael J. Strange

"Let every man or woman here, if you never hear me again, remember this, that if you wish to be great at all, you must begin where you are and with what you are. He who would be great anywhere must first be great in his own Philadelphia."

Russell H. Conwell,
Founder of Temple University

Cryptologic Technician (Collection) 1st Class (EXW) Michael J. Strange hailed from the historic city of Philadelphia. Many rightfully consider the city of Boston as the "cradle of liberty", but it is also true that the city on the banks of the Schuylkill River played a critical role in securing the nation's freedom. Today, the city of Philadelphia looks very different from the time when men like Franklin and Lafayette walked its streets, but despite the centuries that have passed, the city continues to produce patriots who are willing to defend the nation in times of peril.

As a young man, Michael attended the local parochial school and played football and baseball for the local youth organizations. Summers were spent crabbing and fishing with his family on Delaware's eastern shore. By his senior year at North Catholic High, he had made the decision to join the service and two months after graduation, he enlisted in the U.S. Navy.

After basic training Michael was sent to the Center for Information Dominance in Pensacola, Florida, and in April 2005, he reported to the Navy Information Operations Command in Kunia, Hawaii. In May of 2009 he joined an East Coast-based SEAL team in a support role. Navy Seal teams are known for achieving the impossible by using a unique combination of courage, competency and physical stamina to accomplish their missions. However, in addition to being competent in the combat skills needed to survive on the battlefield, these intrepid warriors also require timely critical information in order to achieve success. It was in this area that Petty Officer Strange's skills and talents were applied. As a cryptologic technician, it was his job to provide and protect indispensable intelligence, intelligence that had the capacity to not only allow his team to achieve its mission, but to also save lives.

In August 2011, he would find himself supporting his comrades-in-arms in Afghanistan. During this time, Michael's fellow service members would note that he was a hard worker, physically fit, and a real credit to the United States Navy. On August 6th, Petty Officer

Strange's team was called upon to participate in a mission aimed at interdicting an insurgent attack on U.S. forces. As the team's helicopter neared the designated landing zone, it took a direct hit from an insurgent fired rocket propelled grenade. Michael, along with 29 members of his team and 8 Afghans, was killed making it the deadliest single loss for U.S. forces in the decade-long war in Afghanistan.

Michael would leave behind a loving family and fiancée, and a host of wonderful memories of better and simpler times at places like the rugby field at North Catholic High and Chink's Steaks, a local Philly cheesesteak emporium. Like so many inspiring service members, his service and sacrifice not only defined his life but even more so defined the legacy and tradition of those who consistently answer the call to defend our nation in dangerous and unpredictable times.

Michael Strange was a true native of Philadelphia, an accomplished athlete and a consummate cryptologic professional. Most of all his life was a testament to those indelible principles and attributes that ensure that our nation will continue to be a beacon of freedom and liberty for generations to come.

CTR1 Michael J. Strange
U.S. Navy
June 6, 1986 – August 6, 2011

Photos courtesy of the USN
Narrative - Patrick Weadon, Curator, National Cryptologic Museum
Graphics/Layout - NSA Creative Imaging

Visit our web site, http://www.nsa.gov
MEMORIAL 2011

Appendix B

THE WHITE HOUSE

WASHINGTON

September 23, 2011

Mr. Charles W. Strange, Jr.

█████████████████████

Dear Charlie:

I was deeply saddened to learn of the loss of your son, Petty Officer First Class Michael J. Strange, USN, and it was a solemn honor to join in saluting him as he returned home to his final resting place. Our Nation will not forget his sacrifice, and we can never repay our debt to your family.

A simple letter cannot ease the pain of losing a child, but I hope you take solace in knowing that his brave service exceeded all measures of selflessness and devotion to this country. We pay tribute to him not only as a guardian of our liberty, but also as the true embodiment of America's spirit of service to a cause greater than ourselves.

Michelle and I offer our heartfelt sympathy, and pray that God's grace gives you comfort as you grieve. In life, your son was a shining example of all that is best in our land. In rest, may he find the peace we all seek.

Sincerely,

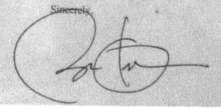

Appendix C

Appendix D

10. (U//FOUO) *Post Investigation Requirements.* I provided the investigation report to the Commander, US Central Command, for his further consideration and evaluation. Once approved, I will ensure relevant stakeholders are informed and will coordinate to provide a detailed family brief. *didut provide the families with the truth.*

11. (U//FOUO) The point of contact for this action is the undersigned at [(b)(2), (b)(6)].

Appendix E

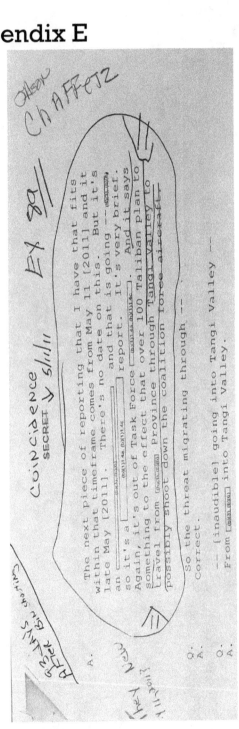

A. The next piece of reporting that I have that fits within that timeframe comes from May 11 [2011] and it's late May [2011]. There's no date on this. But it's an [REDACTED] (b)(1)1.4c and that is going -- [REDACTED] so it's a [REDACTED] (b)(1)1.4c report. It's very brief. And it says Again, it's out of Task Force [REDACTED] (b)(1)1.4c. And it says something to the effect that over 100 Taliban plan to travel from [REDACTED] (b)(1)1.4c Province through Tangi Valley to possibly shoot down the coalition force aircraft.

Q. So the threat migrating through. -- Correct.

A. -- [inaudible] going into Tangi Valley --
Q. From [REDACTED] (b)(1)1.4c into Tangi Valley.
A.

Appendix F

(S//REL TO USA, FVEY) Insurgents Ahsan and Madraz may have been located near with or near the shooters, but Taleban insurgent Ayubi had reportedly fired the round which hit the helicopter. Insurgents may have been coordinating with the Taleban shadow governor for Wardak Province, who was in Pakistan, following the shoot-down, and may have planned to increase vigilance but continue with unspecified plans for a group in Sayyidabad (3356N 06840E), Wardak Province. As well, insurgents near the raid and shoot-down sites may have had IED in place to use against coalition forces which remained in the area. Insurgents may have been receiving information about coalition forces movements from at least one local resident. Insurgents in this group have been associated with [(b)(2), (b)(6)] and [(b)(2), (b)(6)].

Appendix G

AIRCRAFT COMMANDER: From our perspective the ground team was not in any danger, and this will come out later in our discussion, but this insertion was infilling to the follow on HLZ as [(b)(3), (b)(6)] was conducting the call out on the 60 series building separated by two and half clicks. So this was a follow on tasking, not a QRF to help support their situation, it was just a follow on tasking. That is from our perspective, which is what we believe was the case.

[handwritten margin notes:] RMSOS? No? DANGER. WHY SEND SEAL Team

Appendix H

SME GFN1: At any time when you came and checked in and got the handover from [(b)(3), (b)(6)] or [(b)(3), (b)(6)] on the squirters, did they talk about the condition of the LZ or the area surrounding it at all? *NO oNe Checked LANdiNg*

PB65FS: Honestly, sir, I don't think anybody had really looked at the LZ. I mean, at any time if we would have found these squirters, or they would have found weapons, we were -- the way -----

Appendix I

stay on Lefty Grove to facilitate that call-out. That

coordination probably could have gone better -- could have been

better and I think -- I'm not sure, it just appeared to us the

whole plan for getting into this area was rushed, I guess. I — *X##* why

don't know if that's the case, but that's kind of one thing that

I thought might have been done a little bit better.

NAVIGATOR: One of the other things that we did talk about --

kind of what you're hitting on, sir, is about the fact that, you

know, for three hours we had been burning holes in the sky. *3 HOUR'S ?? FLYING*

You've got AWT flying around, so there's a lot of noise going on *AROUND..*

and basically, this entire valley knows that there's something

happening in this area. So, to do an infil on the X or Y, you

know, having that element of surprise in the beginning of an

operation is good, but by the time we've been there for three *IT WAS A*

hours, and the party's up, bringing in another air craft like *1965 Chinook*

that, you know, may not be the most tactically sound decision. *REFURBISHED IN 1985*

TELEVISION SENSOR OPERATOR: At this point, [(b)(3),(b)(6)] already

sent a team to interdict those two squirters down by his

Appendix J

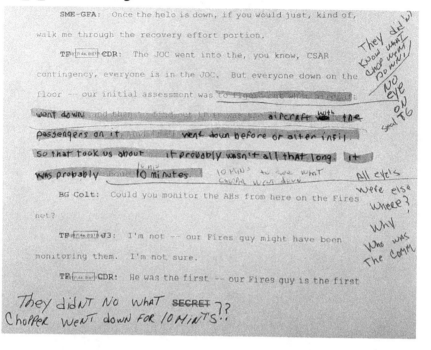

SME-GFA: Once the helo is down, if you would just, kind of, walk me through the recovery effort portion.

TF████CDR: The JOC went into the, you know, CSAR contingency, everyone is in the JOC. But everyone down on the floor -- our initial assessment was ~~to figure out what aircraft~~ went down ~~and then to find out there was the~~ aircraft with the passengers on it, ~~and if it~~ went down before or after infil. So that took us about it probably wasn't all that long. It was probably ~~about~~ 10 minutes. *[handwritten: 10 MINS]* *[handwritten: 10 MINS to see what chopper went down]*

BG Colt: Could you monitor the AHs from here on the Fires net?

TF████J3: I'm not -- our Fires guy might have been monitoring them. I'm not sure.

TF████CDR: He was the first -- our Fires guy is the first

[handwritten margin notes:] They didn't know what chop went down! NO eye on seal T6 — All eyes were else where? Why Who was the comm

[handwritten bottom:] They didNT NO WhaT SECRET?? ChoPPer WeNT dowN FOR 10 MiNTS!!

Endnotes

1   Brown, Don. *Call Sign Extortion 17: The Shoot-Down of SEAL Team Six.* Guilford, Connecticut: Lyons Press, 2015. https://www.amazon.com/dp/B00Y-IRNR4W.

2   Gates, Robert Michael. *Duty: Memoirs of a Secretary at War.* New York: Random House, 2014. https://www.amazon.com/dp/B00F8F3J2S

3   ibid

4   Unruh, Bob. "NSA, CIA Sued for SEAL Team 6 Disaster Details." *WND*, August 23, 2014. https://www.wnd.com/2014/08/nsa-cia-sued-for-seal-team-6-disaster-details/.

5   Shinkman, Paul D. "Obama 'Put a Target on Their Backs', SEAL Team 6 Family Members Say." *U.S. News & World Report*, Mya 2013. https://www.usnews.com/news/articles/2013/05/09/obama-put-a-target-on-their-backs-seal-team-6-family-members-say.

6   "Afghan Helicopter Crash Victim's Remains to Return Home." CBS News, August 8, 2011. https://www.youtube.com/watch?v=j72Q6iX_CG4.

7   Scarborough, Rowan. "Questions about Navy Officer's Cremation Deepen Mystery of Chinook Crash in Afghanistan." *Washington Times*, November 3, 2013. https://www.washingtontimes.com/news/2013/nov/3/questions-about-navy-officers-cremation-deepen-mys/.

8   Polaneczky, Ronnie. "This Philly High School Lost 64 Grads in Vietnam. Now It Will Have a New Life." *Philadelphia Inquirer*, November 9, 2018. https://www.inquirer.com/philly/columnists/ronnie_polaneczky/veterans-day-edison-high-school-vietnam-war-killed-in-action-20181109.html.

9   Vaughn, Billy, Monica Morrill, and Cari Blake. *Betrayed: The Shocking True Story Of Extortion 17 As Told By A Navy SEAL's Father.* Molon Labe Publishing, 2013. https://www.amazon.com/dp/B00G8Q849O/.

10 Campisi, Jon. "Lawyer Files Suit Challenging NSA Phone Record Collection." *Legal Newsline*, June 11, 2013. https://legalnewsline.com/stories/510515500-lawyer-files-suit-challenging-nsa-phone-record-collection.

11 Anonymous SEAL

12 Bunch, Will. "Philly Dad behind NSA Lawsuit: 'Every Day, You Feel Sad.'" *Philadelphia Inquirer*, December 18, 2013. https://www.inquirer.com/philly/news/20131218_Torresdale_dad_behind_NSA_lawsuit___Every_day_you_feel_sad_.html.

13 Kenneth R. Timmerman. "About Kenneth R. Timmerman." Accessed November 10, 2021. http://www.kentimmerman.com/bio.htm.

14 Mitman, Hayden. "Family of Fallen Philly SEAL Meets 'the Trumpster.'" *Metro Philadelphia*, June 26, 2017. https://metrophiladelphia.com/family-of-fallen-philly-seal-meets-the-trumpster/.

15 Forrest, Ben. "Remembering the Fallen." *Vertical Mag*, November 2016. https://verticalmag.com/news/remembering-the-fallen/.

16   Keating, Susan. "Father of Fallen SEAL Team 6 Member Helps Other Grieving Gold Star Parents in Honor of Son: 'We're All the Same.'" *People*, August 10, 2017. https://people.com/human-interest/father-of-fallen-seal-team-6-member-helps-other-grieving-gold-star-parents-in-honor-of-son-were-all-the-same/.

17   "Tony Luke's." Accessed November 10, 2021. https://tonylukes.com/.

18   Keating, Susan. "Father of Fallen SEAL Team 6 Member Helps Other Grieving Gold Star Parents in Honor of Son: 'We're All the Same.'" *People*, August 10, 2017. https://people.com/human-interest/father-of-fallen-seal-team-6-member-helps-other-grieving-gold-star-parents-in-honor-of-son-were-all-the-same/.

CPSIA information can be obtained
at www.ICGtesting.com
Printed in the USA
BVHW081425060122
625106BV00002B/4